MESSAGES
from HEAVEN

MESSAGES *from* HEAVEN

Amazing Insights on
Life After Death, Life's
Purpose and Earth's Future

PATRICIA KIRMOND

SUMMIT UNIVERSITY 🌀 PRESS®

MESSAGES FROM HEAVEN
Amazing Insights on Life After Death, Life's Purpose and Earth's Future
by Patricia Kirmond
Copyright © 1999 Summit University Press.

Library of Congress Catalog Card Number: 99-62419
ISBN: 0-922729-44-1

SUMMIT UNIVERSITY 🍂 PRESS®
Summit University Press and 🍂 are registered trademarks.

Printed in the United States of America
04 03 02 01 00 99   6 5 4 3 2 1

Contents

Introduction

THIS IS THE STORY of my husband's extraordinary and unexpected communications with us, his family, since he passed into the heaven-world in April 1995. Over a three-year period, our family witnessed the growth of my husband's soul as he studied with ascended masters in their universities of the spirit and heavenly cities. During this time, he imparted to us many of the truths he is learning there. What is amazing—and thrilling—is that the spiritual teachings he has shared with us surpass anything he understood while on this earth plane and give us a glimpse of heaven we've never had before.

By God's grace, my husband was permitted to answer many of our questions and give us valuable insights into the life beyond. He also taught us how to live life while we are on earth in order to achieve higher levels of spirituality as we continue on our heavenward journey. He warned us about what is coming upon the earth and about how little time we have left to try to prevent the worst portents of prophecy from happening. He told us how important service is and how his heartfelt desire to be of service to his fellow men and women in his life helped him to balance some of what he had done that was not correct. This dedication to service is what made it possible for him to study in the etheric retreat,[1] where he is at the time of this writing.

In spite of the thrill of receiving these messages, this has not been an easy book for me to compile. It involves the memories of the unhappiest time in my life when my husband of over fifty years unexpectedly made his transition into a higher realm. I thought I was pretty well through the grieving process, but as I started to relive the days and hours before he died in preparation for writing the first part of this book, a great sadness welled up within me. Tears flowed as I brought up those memories that even today are difficult for me to contemplate. Even so, I am grateful for the opportunity to share these messages with those of you who may be led to read this book.

It was exciting for us to receive these communications—such as when a relative goes on a trip to exotic parts of the world and you look forward to the cards and letters telling you all about it. But since this was a two-way communication, it was more like receiving long-distance telephone calls from a traveler or like having a device in your ear that allows you to hear someone giving you instructions that no one else can hear.

During this period, our family was allowed to ask questions, some of which my husband answered and others he said he was not allowed to comment on. Occasionally the answer was just silence. Often he would open by saying something like, "Today I want to talk about the rosebud." Then would come a whole teaching on the opening and expansion of the heart, which he likened to a rose, or some other exposition on an equally profound subject.

My husband often spoke to us about world conditions and his concern for the earth. He was a little sad that some people seemed more interested in having him describe what it was like where he was than in trying to save the planet or in receiving teachings that might help them to grow spiritually.

Messages from Heaven is the distillation of these messages. They started immediately after my husband's death in April 1995 and continued through April 1998. Summit University Press originally published them as a series of three small books entitled *A Special Dispensation*. A wealth of spiritual knowledge was given forth throughout those three years, much to our amazement, for, while my husband had been religious and had a great love for God, he had been a very practical and down-to-earth man—not at all someone we would expect to be giving us advanced teachings once he had left this plane. In his life on earth he had a wonderful sense of humor and would often make jokes about what he considered to be a far-out spiritual idea or belief we had.

In the beginning, we usually received brief messages and comments. We believed that our communication would only continue for a short time, while my husband was in transition, so to speak. We never doubted it was he, as his personality was evident in everything he said. But, even though we were excited to hear from him, we had some concerns about whether it was lawful for him to communicate with us in this way. On several occasions, our daughter, who has always been very protective of her father, said to him, "Dad, are you sure it's all right for you to speak to us like this?"

My husband was a Roman Catholic, though he was open to the idea of reincarnation. He also belonged to the Keepers of the Flame Fraternity, an organization of people who vow to keep the flame of life on earth. I am a member of a nondenominational church that embraces the mystical teachings of the world's major religions. It was founded by the saints of East and West known as the ascended masters, who, like Jesus and Elijah, have become one with God and dwell in higher realms forever. As a group, they are called the Great White Brotherhood, not with any racial implication but because their purified auras are white. Their teachings are given to the world through a specially trained person called a 'messenger.'

As we kept getting more and more information from my husband, I asked the Messenger about it. She was also surprised that the communication was continuing, so she consulted with the ascended masters. The masters told her that my husband was being given a special dispensation to speak to us from the heaven-world because of the serious challenges to the planet through the year 2002 and beyond and the grave situations we face.

Permission for this type of communication is rarely given for an unascended soul, because until a soul is fully ascended it is very easy for error to creep in to what he or she is trying to say. Most "messages" we hear about are from the astral (or lower) plane or from the lower levels of the heaven-worlds. Scripture warns us to beware of this kind of communication, because it usually comes from a level where all is not yet perfected and error still exists. Once a soul has ascended, his or her consciousness, while still individual, participates fully in the consciousness of God and communicates from that level.

Our family will probably never know the full purpose of this dispensation until we are in the higher planes ourselves. But we feel, from the little we have been told, that one reason it has been allowed is that, we who have been the receivers on this side, have always prayed for discernment of spirits and have never been involved in the psychic or astral level of communication. Also, a strong bond has always existed among our souls.

From the point of view of the ascended masters, I imagine

that this was a chance worth taking. They hoped that someone who had so recently been among us could reach the people with the practical truth of the desperate situation of the planet.

While this communication is very exciting, and friends often think it must be wonderful to have this experience and that I shouldn't feel so lonely, I must confess that I do miss my husband as much as anyone would miss a husband or wife. As long as we live in the physical plane, nothing can take the place of the physical presence of someone we love. All who have lost someone very close to them know this.

Nevertheless, this dispensation has been such a wonderful and uplifting experience for our family. To learn more about the heaven-world than we have ever known before, and to have the facts we already knew validated, is a great reward. But to know that my husband's soul is learning and growing at such an accelerated rate is the greatest reward of all. Our cup truly runneth over and our gratitude to our Father/Mother God is endless.

CHAPTER ONE

Our Story

SPRING WAS STARTING to poke its head out from under the heavy blanket of a Rocky Mountain winter as we rushed my husband to the hospital that day—a two-and-a-half hour drive from our home. We had gone to see his doctor that morning, a visit we'd looked forward to because the doctor had been out of town for two weeks and we'd become a little concerned about my husband's condition.

Earlier that month, he'd been in the hospital for five days with pneumonia. He was finally sent home with oxygen, which he was told to use for ten days or so while he recuperated. But three weeks had gone by and he still needed the oxygen. We were beginning to wonder if the doctor might put him back in the hospital but hoped that wouldn't be necessary.

Amidst all of this distraction, it was my husband's birthday and our daughter was flying in to celebrate with us. Eighty years young! Even the doctor couldn't believe my husband was that age, as he was a very active, mentally sharp, in-charge man who looked much younger than his years.

After studying the new chest x-rays, the doctor became extremely alarmed. He directed us to drive immediately to a hospital that has the best medical care in the state. We made a detour, picked up our daughter at the airport and headed out of town.

Once my husband was settled into his hospital room, the doctors assured him that this was something they could handle, and we all began to relax. They just needed to discover what virus or bacteria was causing the lung infection and then find the right antibiotic. And since there were three pulmonary specialists on the case, we felt reassured and confident that all would be well. In fact, my husband felt so much better that when our daughter told him about the small birthday cake she had baked and brought with her on the plane, he decided to have a piece. We had a little celebration in his room. He even had gifts to open, for she had done my gift shopping as well as her own, since with his illness I hadn't been able to get out much.

After the birthday party, my husband was doing so well that, with the doctor's approval, my daughter and I returned to my home for the night so I could secure the house and pack some clothes in preparation for a stay in a motel near the hospital.

When we returned the next day, my husband was complaining about all the tests that they were giving him. He'd also been disturbed by a strange dream he'd had the night before. He dreamt that he had died and that when he tried to contact us we didn't seem to be able to hear him. This made him very frustrated, as there were things he needed to tell us. We made light of his dream, determined not to allow any negative thoughts to influence us. Also, we felt reassured by the doctor's optimism. In the midst of all that was happening, we forgot about the dream. It wasn't until I started to work on this book that I remembered it and understood its significance.

We settled into the motel and hospital routine. The doctors seemed very optimistic. After several days, our daughter returned to her home and job, as she had important commitments and it didn't seem necessary for her to miss them. Ten days later, I again returned home briefly to pick up mail and some other things. When I got back to the hospital, I found my husband sitting up in a chair a little annoyed that I had taken so long to get back. I gave him the mail; he went through it, asked for the checkbook and began paying bills. Then we went for a walk in the halls. He seemed cheerful, waving to the nurses as we went by. By then his oxygen had been turned down to the lowest setting, so he thought he'd soon be off of it entirely. We talked about when he might be allowed to return to our home, and he decided it would probably be a few more days.

This was on a Friday—our most optimistic day since my husband entered the hospital. But by Friday night he started having extreme chills and a fever. His condition went downhill from there. I was shocked to see the change in him, just when he had been doing so well. I wondered if he could have picked up a new infection from something in the hospital. I phoned our daughter and she flew back the next day. I stayed all night in my husband's hospital room, hoping I could be of some help, as his body alternated between burning up with fever and shaking with chills. For the first time, he began to get worried and to wonder if he was going to make it. The doctors busied themselves trying to find the right antibiotic for this new infection.

By Saturday night, my husband seemed a little better. The chills and fever had gone down, and we were encouraged. Around midnight, we went back to our motel room, hoping to get a good night's rest. My daughter fell asleep within a few minutes. But I felt that, as tired as I was, I needed to do some healing prayers for my husband before I could go to sleep.

I went into the bathroom so I wouldn't disturb my daughter. I took my book (I have a large binder filled with prayers for every situation) and let myself be guided as to which prayers to give. When I saw the pattern emerging from the prayers, I suddenly remembered that a friend had told me about a new ritual called "soul retrieval" that had recently been given in our church. I realized that I had been giving the very prayers that were used in that service. All I knew about soul retrieval was that it was important for the healing of the soul because, when our souls go through traumatic experiences, they become shattered and fragmented. This fragmentation causes some of the pieces to be lost. To regain our wholeness we need to gather these lost pieces back to our soul. The process of soul retrieval can act like a magnet to draw back these lost fragments.

I had no idea whether this would work for my husband or not. But I had such a strong feeling that God wanted me to do this that I had to proceed. I let myself be guided as to which prayers I should give, and I asked God to heal him.

These prayers went on for two hours. As I got into it,

I started to feel a burning sensation in the center of my chest. This burning gradually extended throughout my body and intensified until it felt like my whole body was on fire. It began to frighten me, and I wondered for a minute if I were going to burst into flames like those strange cases of spontaneous combustion I had occasionally read about. At the same time, I laughed at myself for thinking such a thing.

Around 2:00 a.m., I finished the service and returned to my bed. It was warmed by the heat from my body, as if I had an electric blanket turned on high. I decided that this must surely mean that my husband was being healed, so I relaxed and went to sleep.

Two hours later, we were awakened by a phone call saying that my husband's lungs were failing and he was being taken to intensive care. We dressed and rushed to the hospital.

When we were finally allowed to see my husband in ICU, he seemed to be doing pretty well with the various medical procedures that were being administered to him. And he was so much better the next morning that he thought they might not keep him in ICU. It was very expensive, and since he was doing so much better, he reasoned, they couldn't justify keeping him there.

Toward the end of the day, his condition started deteriorating again. The doctors decided to put him on life support, as they were still hopeful that some of the medication they were giving him might work, given a little more time. However, from that moment on he never regained consciousness. My son-in-law and another family member arrived too late to communicate with my husband, though they were there to support us when we really needed it. A priest came and gave him the last rites. A minister from my church also came to help in any way he could. After exhausting every effort to help my husband, we all went out to get something to eat.

While I was sitting in the restaurant I felt a cold chill run through my body. I didn't tell anyone, but I wondered what it meant. I guess I really knew what it meant. When we made a brief stop at the motel before returning to the hospital, there was a message for us to come to ICU right away. Then I knew for sure what the chill had meant.

We wanted to say some prayers out loud to help my husband through his transition from this world to the next, but we didn't see how we could do it in his ICU cubical without bothering other people. When we arrived, a very kind young man informed us that the other two patients had been moved to a different section of ICU and there was no one but my husband left in the wing. We were thus free to be with him as long as we needed.

As we entered my husband's cubicle, I smelled a lovely scent like perfume or flowers. A thought came to my mind that maybe the nurse had sprayed something into the atmosphere, and wasn't that thoughtful of her. Then I suddenly wondered if the aroma could have been left by Mother Mary. I had heard that sometimes people smell roses when she enters a room. When we conferred about this afterward, my daughter said she had smelled the perfume too, but our other two companions had not.

My husband had been devoted to the Blessed Virgin. In fact, he had given a rosary novena to her the whole time he was in the hospital. The image of his rosary beads still on his bedside table stayed with me for a long time. It was not a fancy rosary, but a brown utilitarian one that had been given to him in the armed forces—the kind a soldier would carry into battle.

We all stood around his bed for about forty minutes and did a prayer service to free him from his no-longer-useful body. As we finished our service and were singing a song to Mother Mary, we heard my husband speak. "That was quite a send-off you gave me," he said. We were very excited that he could speak to us, and it brought tears to our eyes.

Then the nurses came back to ICU bringing new patients. We said our good-byes and left. We thought that my husband had probably just been allowed to speak to us as he was leaving the physical plane and that would be the end of it. We were grateful to have this communication and to be assured that our loved one still existed though his body was dead.

We didn't hear from my husband again until we were driving to the town where his cremation service would take place. He said, "I don't think it will take you more than an hour to cut me free, as I'm pretty free already."

This made us cry, but also laugh, as it was so typical of my husband. He was extremely time-oriented. In fact, our daughter often referred to him as "my father, the clock." On that day he wanted to be sure we would be finished in time to eat lunch and then pick up relatives at the airport.

The ascended masters teach that the best way to dispose of a body is through cremation. This is because even after death the soul tends to be emotionally attached to the body. And often friends and loved ones hold on to a person after he or she has passed on. Passing the body through the fire is the quickest way to free the soul from its attachments to the physical world.

In our church, cremation is not held until seventy-two hours after death, in order to give the life force a chance to withdraw before the body is consumed. During the cremation service a few loved ones and a minister usually go to witness the cremation while praying for the soul to be cut free to go to higher levels of existence. This isn't at all macabre, but a wonderful spiritual experience. After witnessing the fire consume the body, you know beyond a shadow of a doubt that the body is not the real person.

My husband had participated in several of these services with me; that's how he decided he might like to be cremated. At one time Catholics weren't allowed to be cremated. But in recent years it has become acceptable, and now a number of Catholics are choosing cremation. For me it has always been the natural way, as I come from a family where everyone on my mother's side has been cremated for three generations. Of course, they didn't witness the cremation the way we do in our church.

Fifteen people attended my husband's cremation—a crowd in that small room. After exactly one hour had passed, we all felt that our work was done and that we could leave. A few days later, two memorial services were held, one at the Catholic Church and another at the chapel in the community where we live. My husband had been helpful to so many people in our community. He was a person who was knowledgeable about many things, so he'd helped people with their real estate problems, small legal matters, financial issues and anything else they needed assistance with. No matter how tired he was, he never turned anyone away. It seemed that many of our neighbors would miss him almost as much as I would.

As I sat in the front row of the chapel during the memorial service in our community, feeling the love and care flowing from so many people, I suddenly thought I saw my husband standing in front of me. Then he knelt and put his arms around me. He was very shimmery, not solid looking. He seemed to be clothed in blue and white, almost as if he were wearing a uniform. For a minute I thought this was really happening, but then, as he faded away, I decided it was probably just my imagination.

Some months later, when he was communicating with us often, I happened to think to ask my husband about his memorial service. He said that he had indeed attended that service, that he had knelt before me and placed his arms around me.

This confirmation was important to me, as it's so easy to dismiss spiritual visions as being just a figment of one's imagination. I've seen him in the same shimmering form at other times since then, usually when I'm at a spiritual service. At these times he appears as he did when he was in his thirties.

After my husband's life had been sealed by the three services that were held for him, we started to hear from him again. We had been so hopeful that he would live, and so puzzled when he died, that we had an autopsy performed on his body. The cause of death was sepsis, or what used to be called blood poisoning. We asked him if it would have made any difference in his passing if we had taken him to a different hospital. His answer was, "No matter which hospital you would have taken me to, I feel that this was to be the final chapter of my life. I do not have the feeling that I would have lived longer, except by divine intervention."

CHAPTER TWO

The Earliest Messages

IN THE BEGINNING, we usually received short messages from my husband. We didn't bother to record them, as they often came to us in the midst of other activities. Though several times he suggested that we write these messages down, somehow it just never happened. Finally one day, he said, "The masters are getting annoyed with you. If you don't start writing these messages down, they aren't going to allow me to talk to you any more!" We "got the message," and from that moment we began recording everything he said. We also started a more formalized communication process of meditating and praying for at least thirty minutes before we asked my husband if he had anything to say—to be sure that we were in the right vibration to hear him correctly. This is when we began receiving longer messages and teachings.

While all the communications from him are interesting, you

may notice as you read his early messages that he quickly begins to grow in his understanding and his ability to teach. By the last half of the book, the vibration of the teachings is at a much higher level than it was when he began. This doesn't mean that his beginning messages weren't of value, but they are a yardstick by which we can measure the growth of a soul who is studying and being tutored in an etheric retreat.

The nature of heaven

My husband told us that when he first arrived on the other side he was surprised to see how busy everyone was. A big orientation was in progress for souls who were being shown what they had and had not accomplished in the life they had just finished. They were told to go to the right side or to the left side, depending on whether they were to make their ascension or to re-embody. My husband was sent to neither side but was left in the middle. At the time we didn't understand the significance of this, but it became apparent to us later on.

He also commented on how life was organized in heaven:

> *Things are very orderly here. There is a plan. Much work seems to be done by teams that support different evolutions of life on many systems of worlds. It is more beautiful and peaceful here than you can imagine, and yet this is a busy place. I keep learning and learning and learning. We are just exposed to the tip of the iceberg on earth. We do not begin to access all that is possible for us to have—this takes the Christ Mind.*

He also mentioned that "you remember everything you are taught." We thought how wonderful it would be if *we* could remember everything we'd been taught on earth!

The value of service

One of the first special teachings my husband gave us was on the value of service:

> *I can't emphasize enough the importance of service— helping others. Service that is given from the heart is the equivalent of money in heaven! I am so grateful for every time I helped someone, because this is part of the reason that I am allowed to study at this retreat.*
>
> *It helps you tremendously to have served life. Service transforms the server. Purely motivated service is like light. The earth needs more souls who are willing to serve and fewer who are so willing to judge. People should look for ways to serve and not ways to be served.*

This one message has brought about great change in the attitudes of many people who have read it. It helps us understand that service actually transforms the server. But service must be given from the heart—not grudgingly because we feel we have to.

He also said, "Love should be our immediate response to all people. Not judgment—not hatred—not envy—only love."

The condition of the planet and its future

We asked my husband about the condition of our country and the world. His answer was:

> *What strikes me is that most of us, including me while I was on earth, cannot see the handwriting on the wall. I knew that many things were deteriorating, but I was too caught up in day-to-day living to feel and see what in many ways is very visible.*

The nation is experiencing a time similar to when the Roman Empire crumbled and when the continent of Atlantis sank. People's senses grow dull. They do not feel the deterioration of the basic moral fiber of the nation, or they feel it and do not know what to do about it.

Yet the masters have not given up hope. What they require is an equation of light, a certain ratio of light to darkness to counteract the darkness. It is so small compared to what you might think.

A few months after my husband's death, we asked him about earth's future and what he could tell us from his vantage point about the possibility of cataclysm.

I knew that earth was in some peril when I was in embodiment, but I did not begin to realize how bad things have gotten. It's as if the earth has become a matter for spiritual engineers. They are working at inner levels to try to secure the foundation of a crumbling edifice. I do not feel that you will avoid all cataclysm, but you still have time to change the worst portents.

It is hard for people to comprehend the level of sacrifice that is needed now so that the worst can be avoided later. People grow tired. They doubt the path. They want to hear happy messages.

One has only to study the conditions on this planet to realize how accurate the ascended masters have been—and are at this time. There is such opportunity ahead if people will sacrifice now.

When we asked what else he would have us know, my husband replied:

Life is meant to be lived for God. You know how in real estate we say that the three most important things are "location, location and location"? Well, <u>we</u> should think they are "God, God and God." We should always ask ourselves: Is this God's will? Would God approve of this? Will God be honored by this action?

Life would be much simpler, much less painful and far more peaceful if we did this. We have lost our center, which is God. If we do not return to this center, the consequences will be disastrous.

The comment about real estate was natural for my husband. He had a very successful twenty-year career in real estate after retiring from the army.

We noticed that when we gave my husband his choice of a topic, he usually chose something more serious to speak about. We appreciated these messages very much, but every once in a while our curiosity got the better of us, and we tried to get him to answer what we called a "fun" question.

Do you eat meals in heaven?

Good food and regular meals were always very important to my husband, a legacy from the French side of his family and from the five years we lived in Paris. So we were curious to hear his answer to this question, as we were sure he would have something interesting to say on the subject.

Our meals are spectacular! We drink many juices that are like the pure essence of any fruit or vegetable you can imagine. Everything we consume seems light, not heavy or dense in any way.

> *We do eat regular meals and have occasional banquets. Most of the food is different from anything we were used to on earth—and ten times better! Eating does not take on great importance but is part of the ritual of this retreat and does seem to be enjoyed.*

The body temple

We end this chapter with the first fairly long teaching my husband gave us. It's on caring for our bodies—our holy temples, he calls them—as basic to living a balanced spiritual life.

> *Today I wish to speak to you about the holy temple. The body is meant to be treated as a temple. This requires attention to diet, exercise, spiritual practice, general hygiene and appearance.*
>
> *Imagine that you worked for an ascended master. How would you show up for work each day? In reality, God should be your first employer; then you would see your earthly employer with more balance.*
>
> *Diet affects the state of health of your entire body. For you to have a healthy diet takes knowledge of nutrition and attunement to your own needs. The macrobiotic diet, for example, is excellent, but it calls for substantial adaptation for each person, the West being different from the East in a way that many do not account for.*
>
> *Exercise gives energy to your cells. It is like a boost. It is not indulgent but necessary for your body to hold the maximum light. Twenty minutes a day will suffice, but it should not be neglected.*
>
> *When something is holy we treat it with respect and care.*

We honor it and are grateful to have it in our midst. So it should be with our temples. They house the living spirit. If we do not care for them, they deteriorate with a vengeance.

We should be living longer and stronger than we are. My body simply gave out; I could no longer fight the battle. It had served me well, but I can now see that I did many things that hindered rather than helped it.

I should never have smoked, drunk coffee or liquor, and I should have consumed far less fat. In general, I had a strong constitution and this is an extra blessing along the path. I did, however, misuse my energy due to my own unresolved psychology. I was impatient with many situations, and I did get myself into stressful states by how I overworked myself, worried or reacted.

One way to honor the holy temple of the body is to address anything that is out of alignment. It is like the princess and the pea; you cannot shut the door on your psychology and think that you are living in harmony with the law. It is like putting a cover on a volcano; it will ultimately erupt and cause more damage than if it had been freed.

Spiritual practice is the driving force that helps propel light through the body. It nourishes the cells. It provides holiness when the system is ready to be holy. It must be genuine. It must be purely motivated. It must be desired, not imposed. It should be a constant in a person's life.

Attention to hygiene and appearance is simply respecting the vehicle you have been given. "Cleanliness is next to Godliness" is true. When you have the choice to be clean and to make the most of your appearance, this is the right thing to do.

However, if these concerns dominate your time or thought, then things are out of balance.

Light gives the person more beauty than anything that could ever be purchased. However, it is lawful to look nice and represent God wherever you go. Also, cleanliness keeps earthbound spirits from becoming attached to you and sapping your light or strength.

CHAPTER THREE

An Experience of Transition

WE HAD BEEN WAITING for my husband to tell us more about his transition, but he hadn't volunteered anything on the subject. So we decided to ask him about his experience, and what a wonderful story came forth!

What happened at the time of your transition?

I am being permitted to share with you only a portion of my spiritual journey since leaving planet earth. I must tell things as I have seen and understood them, and this may be challenging for some who read this.

I did not pass through a tunnel as in the near-death experiences. But then mine was not a near-death experience. I was greeted by a magnificent angelic being who welcomed me by my first name and stated that he would be accompanying

me on my journey. There are bands of angels who help specifically with the transition of lightbearers.[2]

I did ask him some questions. I asked if this meant that
I would not be returning. I expressed concern for my family.
I could simultaneously look back at my body and see that it
could no longer provide a home for me. Everything was clear
to me. I was not confused like people are who die in accidents
or totally unexpectedly.

There is a freedom you experience that makes you realize just how formfitting and restricting the body is. And yet we
must be grateful for our bodies and treat them with respect, as
we need them to progress.

I did watch you give your final prayers over my body.
And I was permitted to speak with you at that time. I was so
pleased that you could hear me, but I did not yet know that this
would continue.

So much flashed before me, and I wished so deeply that
I had put more things in place for the family before I moved
on. The angel assured me that you would be able to manage
and that you would be protected and guided. He embodied the
comfort flame along with a presence of love and gentle wisdom.
I could not doubt anything in his presence.

Meeting with Mother Mary

Before being taken to my place on the etheric level, I was
greeted by Mother Mary. She said, "Welcome, my son," and
thanked me for doing her rosary. I was amazed that she would
be thanking me. In her presence one has the feeling of being
enveloped by the highest sense of a mother's love that you can

imagine. I felt as if her very being had somehow healed my soul for the journey ahead. She is the one who placed the scent of flowers in my intensive care cubicle after I died.

Mother Mary is revered even in heaven for her numerous attempts to intercede for this planet. Her rosary is like a magnet that pulls down heaven's intercession. You must not neglect it. She has not forgotten what it is like to raise children and struggle on this planet. Her warnings should not be ignored. She is so concerned that earth not have to pass through its darkest hours.

Meeting friends and family

I did not immediately see friends and family who had died, as some people do. But I was reunited with some of them later and told where others were. Many souls have, of course, reembodied.

It is my understanding that a soul who does not understand re-embodiment is initially permitted to be reunited with some of his family or friends. Later he is tutored in the concept of reincarnation. At that point he learns who is truly in the etheric or astral realms and who has reembodied. As you know—and I witness this daily here—all things are possible in God.

One of the first souls I was allowed to see was Patrick [a friend who had made his transition just six months earlier]. He looked larger than life to me, taller and filled with light. He was anxious to help me feel oriented, but he also had his wonderful sense of humor intact. We are at very different retreats with different missions to fulfill. This was part of God's mercy and gentle orientation that I could see someone who had so recently been in an environment similar to mine.

This statement affected me greatly because at the time our friend Patrick died I was feeling very sad and imagining how hard it must be for his wife. Suddenly the thought popped into my mind, "What if six months from now my husband were to die? How would I feel?" I shoved the thought away as something negative that was not allowed to be there and forgot about it. My husband's health was quite good then, and there was nothing that worried us. Yet six months later he was dead.

Levels of heaven and hell

The spiritual realm is much more magnificent but also much more complex than I had ever imagined. Yes, there is heaven, but heaven has many layers, levels or octaves. People do not all go to the same location.

If you think about divine justice, how could there be only one heaven and one hell when so many different types of souls walk this earth? Do we not all know at least one person who radiates a spiritual sense that is stronger than most others we have met?

What you find within the category of heaven are different etheric levels with etheric retreats. These retreats are run by angels or ascended hosts.

Within what we have called "hell," there are multiple levels of the astral plane, including hell itself. Each level going down in vibration intensifies in its severity and in the recalcitrance of the souls sent there. In the etheric plane, each level going up in vibration intensifies in its light and in the spiritual purity of the souls there.

Entering the retreat for souls new to heaven

I was first taken to a retreat on the etheric level, which was also an orientation center for newly arrived souls. The absolute love and care given to me was in every way astounding. Think of the highest, most profound spiritual experience you have ever had, and what I have experienced here will most likely be beyond that in every way.

I was given certain baths of light with the violet flame. These were given to raise my vibration and draw my full being into wholeness.

We questioned my husband about these baths. He said that they are prepared by master alchemists to provide the exact amount of blue or pink color in the violet that each soul needs. The ascended masters teach that violet is the wavelength of God's light that transmutes muddy, polluted energy into clear light. [see chapters 4 and 6] Blue is the color of God's will and pink is the color of God's love. Therefore, the blue side of violet would contain more of the aspect of God's will; the pink side would contain more of God's love.

Everyone appears at his best, with more height and a more youthful look than those of us who have just left earth at an advanced age do.

It would seem that, in heaven at least, appearance is a product of consciousness.

The life review

Very early on I was allowed to review my entire life. Everything was so vivid. Every moment spent in anger or impatience or fear or self-pity seemed so wasted. I was instantly made aware of the patterns or momentums, both positive and negative, which had been part of my life. I was so grateful for any time when I had served with an unselfish heart and for the times when I had loved and honored life or made the honest or just choice. I was painfully aware of the ways in which I had wasted energy or blocked my own progress through often foolish but embedded habit patterns.

The basic questions are: How did you use the hours of your life? Essentially, how much of your life have you served God in your fellowman and in your day-to-day actions? How developed is your heart chakra, your capacity to love?

You are allowed to give your own comments on the assessment of your life. This is followed by a meeting with a board of heavenly beings who give their analysis of your life. You are shown past lives where you can see most clearly the origin of many of your habit patterns and the reasons for many of the events that took place in your life. The biblical saying "an eye for an eye" and "a tooth for a tooth" (Exod. 21:24) becomes more real in the context of understanding your past failures and successes.

We each have a recording angel. Nothing is missed. God is not mocked or fooled in any way. We only fool our human self by our actions. And in reality, deep inside the soul always knows what is right or wrong, though many try to deaden themselves to its voice.

During this review of lifetimes I was allowed to know what karma I had needed to balance and what I did balance. The whole tone of the review was loving and positive, not judgmental. It was a time of great learning for my soul.

In many ways you are your own judge, for you can see so clearly where you have erred. I felt highly motivated to get on with what I still needed to transmute. I wished that I had realized many things while I was in embodiment. And now I feel so privileged to be able to share this so that many others may take the opportunity to face themselves while they are still in embodiment.

A helpful exercise for each of you would be to run the film clips of your life, so to speak, and begin to look at how you have been utilizing the hours of your life. Notice the progress you have made. Perhaps you are a totally different person than you were ten years ago. That counts for much in heaven.

Do not get stuck in self-reproach. Make each day count toward the new directions that you want to take. Extra points are given for lessons you have genuinely learned and tests you have passed, even if not on the first try.

I struggle to think of ways to help people keep that daily co-measurement with God. One thing that might help is to remember that everything happens for a reason. There are no coincidences. Therefore, if a difficult person enters your life, do not spend your time condemning him, but rather ask yourself, *What can I learn from this person? What would it take for me not to lose my harmony over this person?* This does not mean that you condone the person's actions, but it does mean that you are alert to the possible test of your balance and harmony.

I did not always see the test when I was in embodiment, and I would get annoyed with various individuals. My salvation was that I never held a grudge or spent hours of my life

*focusing on one person's treatment of me. It is possible to let
one person keep you from your ascension. Ask yourself, is there
anyone that I'm allowing to keep me from my spiritual
progress because I cannot forgive him?*

*Know that I have only shared a small glimpse of the
intricate but magnificent journey that God has prepared for us.*

We had been curious to know what had really happened the
night I did the decrees [see chapter 4] and prayers for soul
retrieval while my husband was in the hospital, so I asked him:

Was I led to do the soul retrieval for my sake or yours?

*It was definitely for me. And this would be a wonder-
ful service for anyone who is critically ill or near death and
who is open to the light of God. It allowed portions of my soul
to be retrieved and a new alignment to occur before my transition. It allowed me to pass from the screen of life with a
greater sense of internal wholeness. This wholeness allowed me
to more readily access all that was in my Causal Body³ and
to suffer only momentary confusion in my transition.*

*The concept of soul retrieval is very much an esoteric or
inner temple teaching. It might be difficult for some to comprehend. The truth is that many life events are shattering to the soul.
Some we impose on ourselves and others are imposed on us.*

*For example, a child who is abused will have this frag-
mentation occur. That is why, even with therapy, without the
understanding and giving of decrees [see chapter 4], it may
take years for such a person to feel whole, and they still may
not feel 100 percent healed. The therapy is critical but not
always sufficient for complete healing to occur.*

Soul retrieval can accomplish a level of healing that few other spiritual practices offer. This, combined with the use of the violet flame [see chapter 4], would be most helpful for the individual who has suffered abuse. I have chosen a dramatic example, but many lesser experiences can also be shattering. Most of us can feel this fragmentation when these incidents occur. This is a sign to you that soul retrieval is necessary.

As to the burning you felt, you were given an infusion of light during the period of your decrees to help sustain you through what was to come. Such is the love of God for the devout soul.

As I meditated on this last statement, I was so very grateful to God for that infusion of light, because I did somehow get through the days following my husband's death rather well. Yet I was not at all prepared for his death and fought it every step of the way. The thought of his no longer being with me was almost more than I could bear. We had met when I was twenty, during the Second World War, and were married within the year. By the time of his death we had celebrated our 50th wedding anniversary. When he died, I truly didn't know who I was for awhile; I had been married to him all of my adult life.

Several months after his death my husband told me that we were twin flames, individual souls who were created together in the beginning as one spirit, but he had not been allowed to tell me until then. This explains a great deal about why we are working together now, and it also explains something he wrote in a letter shortly after our marriage, which I recently found. In that letter he acknowledged that he knew he was going to marry me the first time he saw me. I can't say that I was as attuned to this as he was.

It is said that the angels work very hard trying to unite souls who are meant to be together in their earthly embodiments or even to interact for a short period of time. It's not so difficult when they are born in the same area, but when they embody in different parts of the country or the world, it must become quite a challenge. My husband grew up in the Great Lakes region of the United States, and I lived on the West Coast.

The chances of our meeting would have seemed fairly slim, but the Second World War came along and people, particularly men, were being moved all over the country. Eventually, after numerous transfers, my husband ended up in a town in California where one of my girlfriends was attending college. He decided that the college would be a good place to meet nice girls. He and several other soldiers went there and met an art teacher who introduced them to some of her students. One of these students was my friend, and she started dating one of the soldiers. She invited him to her parents' ranch for a weekend, but he was shy and wouldn't go unless she invited his friend, my future husband. And that's how the angels accomplished their mission, as I reluctantly agreed to help my girlfriend out and go on a blind date with him.

CHAPTER FOUR

More Early Messages

As the weeks progressed and my husband kept giving us more and more material, we were amazed. We finally asked him if he was trying to write a book. This was his response:

> *I am a witness to the glory of God and the ascended masters. I am a witness to the learning of a newly unascended or ascended being. I am a witness to the mission of the Church and its Messenger. I am a witness to the needs of the hour.*
>
> *I am not a book writer, nor do I necessarily propose a book. This is your dharma. What I give is meant to be shared with others in whatever form will be most beneficial.*

As the days passed it became increasingly obvious that a book was in the making. Within six months of my husband's death the first small book was in print in English. It was quickly translated into Spanish, and then into Portuguese and eventually into other languages. Two longer booklets followed over the next two and a half years, and the soul who denied that he was a "book writer" was soon talking about "my first book" and eventually "my third book."

Changing one's mind after death

A request my husband wrote at the time of his heart surgery (two years before he died) and that he changed after his death made me wonder how many people make requests in their wills and, after they make their transition, find that they have been wrong in asking for something that was not God's will. By that time it's too late to amend the request.

My husband was fortunate that he was allowed to speak to us and that what he had written prior to his death was not a legal document. The request I found after his death stated that if he died I was to pay for perpetual masses to be given for him by several Catholic organizations. Also, if I tithed to my church, I had to tithe the same amount to the Catholic Church. The latter concerned me, so we decided to ask him about it. This is what he said:

> You do not need to tithe to the Catholic Church. You may do whatever you like with the money as long as you are wise and somewhat cautious about your choices. You must remember that I have had many lives as a Catholic, and even now as I look upon the Catholic Church, I cannot tell you it is _all_ wrong and that your church is _all_ right. Each could learn something from the other.
>
> There are some dear souls in the Catholic Church. Mother Teresa is not the only saint in the earth. There is, how-

ever, much corruption in the Catholic Church and a desire to keep certain truths from the people.

Perpetual masses are good when done by souls of light to help people who are in transition. For a church with no service particularly dedicated to assisting souls to ascend, these masses are very supportive to the soul. But I do not need the perpetual masses because I now understand a higher teaching and have benefited greatly from the decrees that have been given for me.

Remember, in heaven there are no denominations. Denominations are not necessarily wrong, but when they become divisive and hateful, they lose access to the blessings of God.

We asked this next question because of my husband's strong ties to the Catholic Church and because he always had a tendency to tell priests, in a nice way, how to do their jobs. The question was: "Were you ever a pope?"

No, I was never a pope, but a cardinal three times and a bishop three times.

Giving decrees

At this point I'd like to define briefly the process of decreeing, as my husband mentions it a number of times throughout the book. A prayer is a devout petition or entreaty or a sending of love and thanks to God. A decree is a command or order given in the name of God and the Christ for the will of God to come into manifestation. God gave this authority in Isaiah 45:11 when he said, "Concerning the work of My hands, command ye me." Decrees in our church are rhythmical, poetic mantras that are given aloud, either alone or with a group. The vibratory action of this spiritual practice builds a pool of light for the angels and ascended masters to use. Decrees can be powerful tools to call angels into action in the earth.

We asked my husband what he could tell us about the effects of praying and decreeing.

These are like fuel in your tank. They prevent many negative things from happening while allowing other positive things to happen. We can "look down" and immediately tell those who decree from their hearts. They have an extra light and protection about them.

It is important to know that many people who consider that they are on the spiritual path do not exude this light. They try to hide behind their prayers or decrees and spiritual practices, but they are not honest with themselves or with God.

You cannot gossip one minute and decree or pray the next. You cannot hate and yell in anger one minute and call out to God the next. All of these habits are indications of an unresolved psychology.

How do you work out your psychology on the other side?

It is much harder here. We can see everything, but we are dependent on situations that will allow us to work things out. When you are in embodiment you have constant opportunities to change—to select the higher path, to address your psychology. And yet many remain blinded to their bad habits, as I did.

On this side we must pray for opportunities to serve that will allow us to transcend these momentums. Some of these come through others in our retreat; but sometimes our progress depends on the opportunity to serve all of you. Therefore we need your prayers. This is why some of us have no choice but to re-embody.

No teachings have more practical answers for everyday life than those the ascended masters have given. The retreats themselves are run with a definite sense of practicality. Even though they transcend anything that we have ever known, they are efficient and practical, which you can imagine that I love.

We smiled when my husband made that comment, as we knew him to be a very practical person.

Next he seemed anxious to give us this wonderful teaching on labor:

Labor

We have been talking about labor. I have learned a great deal about the benefits of hard work. The masters help us to see the utter importance of striving for excellence in all that we do, whether it is perfecting a swim stroke, making a phone call or building a house.

If life is meant to glorify God, then the more we strive for excellence, the more we are able to be one with the mind of God. We have never lived at a time when fewer people have been aware of this law. We have become a society of expedience, convenience, deception and harried lives.

Failure is not the problem, but failing to strive for the highest allows the consciousness to accept lesser and lesser standards for day-to-day living. With this comes a general decline.

Modern music and drugs have played a major role in

this mediocrity. Decree for the healing of the music industry. Without decree work, no discourse or investigative report can impact this industry.

I learn so much in a day! What I learn here in a day would require a month of studying to learn on earth. It is magnificent here, but simultaneously I am always aware of the work that needs to be done.

My husband's mention of music reminded us of an interesting experience one member of our family had. She was sitting under a hair dryer in a beauty shop while my husband was talking to her. Suddenly he said, "I can't stay! I can't stay! The music is pushing me away!" She got out from under the dryer and found that someone had tuned the radio to a station that was playing rock music. It was that vibration that had repelled my husband away from the shop. We thought that this music probably has the same effect on angels.

We asked my husband if he would always be able to talk to us like this, and he said no, that this was a special dispensation but it would go on for a time.

When we didn't hear from him for a while, we asked him if he was aware of what we were doing, and also where was his retreat. He answered:

I am well aware of most everything you do. Simultaneously, however, I am a student in a retreat, and I now have some beginning assignments to help with specific projects that our retreat is undertaking.

I am definitely at a retreat in the etheric plane over the North American continent.

The importance of the violet flame

My husband spoke to us of the importance of the violet flame. The violet flame is an action of the Holy Spirit that transmutes negative energy into positive. It helps us transmute our negative karma, the record of negative thoughts, feelings and deeds from other lives as well as this one. He indicated that in heaven people work with the violet flame regularly and said that he wished he had given more violet flame decrees when he was on earth. We smiled at this because he had never wanted to give many violet flame decrees while he was in embodiment. He talks about this flame in detail later on in the book (chapter 6). Through studying in the retreats he truly came to understand and appreciate the qualities of this flame.

A very simple way to invoke the violet flame is to give this mantra a number of times while visualizing spiritual flames of violet hue surrounding your body:

I am a being of violet fire,
I am the purity God desires.[4]

This flame has the power to transmute anything that is negative in your aura. It can also transmute national and world karma, mitigate cataclysm and accelerate spiritual development.

Are you in Saint Germain's retreat?

After some time we asked my husband if he was with the ascended master Saint Germain, as we sensed that he was in a violet-flame retreat. He said yes, he was in Saint Germain's retreat. Saint Germain is the master who introduced the violet flame to spiritual seekers early in this century through the I AM movement.

He will be the master of the coming Aquarian age, just as Jesus was the master of the Piscean age. He also sponsors the United States of America and anchors the light of freedom for the planet. His retreat is in the etheric plane above Table Mountain in Wyoming. He also uses the Grand Teton Retreat located above the Grand Teton Mountain near Jackson Hole, Wyoming.

We commented to my husband that we thought he might have gone to the retreat of Archangel Michael, Mother Mary or Jesus. He said that though he loved these masters very much and his tie to them came naturally, while he was on earth he hadn't comprehended (but needed to learn) the importance of the violet flame. So now one of the things he must do is to bring people to the knowledge of the violet flame.

The cycles of returning karma

My husband wanted to give us an understanding of why people in every nation are dealing with so many disasters and illnesses today.

> *Karma has been descending for centuries, but at no other time has the karma returned so swiftly or so severely, both for the individual and the planet. This is creating many devastating situations for people who do not understand the law of cycles. (New cycles cannot begin until the karma of the previous cycle is cleared.)*

> *You must prepare for some very hard years on a planetary scale. No one will be totally free from cataclysm and earth changes. What remains to be determined is the nature of war and the possible levels of destruction. A major war can still be averted, but the window is closing because fewer people than*

were expected are responding to the needs of the hour with prayers and decrees.

People's spiritual centers are growing weak instead of strong. Their hearts and minds are focused on the details of daily life, on the attainment of human comfortability or, in some cases, on sheer survival.

The most effective way to transmute karma and avert or mitigate cataclysm and war is the use of the violet flame, which will be discussed more fully in chapter 6.

CHAPTER FIVE

A Master's Retreat

AFTER MANY LIFETIMES as a servant of mankind, Saint Germain ascended on May 1, 1694, and began a very unusual sequence of interactions with the people of earth. He was given a special dispensation from the Lords of Karma to reappear from time to time in a physical body.[5] Thus he began a series of unique encounters with eighteenth-century European courtiers,[6] American revolutionaries,[7] and nineteenth- and twentieth-century spiritual seekers[8] over the past 300 years. History records that he met the Countess de Georgy of France in 1710, and when she saw him again in 1767, he had not aged a bit. Madame Adhemar, who met him in 1760, found him un-aged when next she saw him in 1789. Numerous people in the 1700s attempted to follow him, only to discover that he had walked out a door or around a corner and simply disappeared. His mission in those years was to ease the birth pangs of democracy, both in Europe and America. He helped to further the establishment of the American republic, tried to prevent the violence of the French Revolution and inspired the Masons with the mystical vision of an ideal government composed of united but sovereign states.[9]

In the late nineteenth-century, he helped other ascended masters and unascended adepts found the Theosophical Society through Helena P. Blavatsky. In the '30s, he worked with Guy and Edna Ballard to found the I AM movement. In 1958, he and other ascended masters founded The Summit Lighthouse through Mark L. Prophet and, when Mark ascended in 1973, they continued to work through Elizabeth Clare Prophet. Saint Germain is still seen from time to time by those gifted with inner vision, but rarely appears in physical form.[10]

What is it like to be in an ascended master retreat?

The retreat of Saint Germain is like a city of light. It is beyond our earthly imagination in splendor and beauty. It is filled with artwork that lifts the spirit. We hear music that accelerates every erg of energy in our beings.

Seeing the art here makes me realize how low our standards have fallen in the art that is produced on earth. Much of what is sold and exhibited as art simply outpictures the astral plane and the torment of souls who feel trapped because they are separated from God.

At the highest level, art is meant to reconnect man with God and his true identity. Art is also meant to capture the multifaceted aspects of history and life, pain and suffering as well as joy and overcoming. It was never intended to degrade,

*distort, depress or harm the spirit of the person looking at it.
Art captures energy. If you feel a pain in your third eye, in the
center of your forehead, you are not in the presence of anything
that God has inspired. You can tell something about the state of
a planet by the art that is being produced. Judge for yourselves.
What images are we putting before our youth? Do they even
know what is possible?*

*Many of the walls in our retreat are made of thin
layers of precious gems. Our main meeting room has thin
amethyst walls. The beauty is indescribable, and the effect
of light on these walls is magnificent. We have a number of
rooms and images that are violet, in recognition of our mission
to share and outpicture the violet flame. We also have areas
that feature other colors. They are typically iridescent and transcend the hues we are used to on earth.*

*We each have our own rooms, and the color of these
rooms is determined by our own spiritual needs. If we need to
grow on a specific ray, it is often outpictured in the color of the
room to which we are assigned.*

On the organization of Saint Germain's retreat

*The retreat is organized with an efficiency, fluidity and
harmony that is almost unknown to us on earth. So much time
on earth is taken up satisfying people's egos and desires that
little attention is given to the divine plan, the God-solution, and
to organization. If people could let go and let God be the doer
in all aspects of their lives, we would have a golden age.*

*We are allowed to work at our own pace here. People
seem to progress at different rates. We all report to spiritual*

directors who help us with our progress.

I am determined to transmute all that I can in order to move on to the next level of attainment. Some of the other unascended students do not seem as anxious to move forward. This may seem strange, but this retreat contains so much more than we have ever known on earth that it is a bit overwhelming to some. And souls are very unique, both in their attainment and in the momentums they need to overcome.

Until the ascension, there are no guarantees of staying on a specific etheric level unless you continue to transcend yourself. A person arrives at a certain rung of the ladder because he has earned that level, but the maintaining or ascending or descending is up to him. The more mastery you can earn here, the easier it will be to progress if you have to re-embody.

When a person makes his transition, if he is permitted to come to the etheric level, there are four possibilities for his ongoing evolution. These depend on his attainment and the nature of his karma. The first possibility is that he will definitely need to re-embody. The prayer in this case is that he may be born to a family of great light and spiritual understanding.

The second is that he may have to re-embody. But by an extraordinary effort of service and transmutation, he may be permitted to stay in the etheric retreats and become a candidate for the ascension.

The third is that he does not have to re-embody and is definitely a candidate for the ascension, even though the ascension may not take place for some time. The final and most desired possibility is that he makes his ascension and never has to re-embody again.[11]

I am in the second category and will not know for some time whether I will continue here or return to earth. I am, of course, determined to become a candidate for the ascension. And I am anxious for all of you to arrive here in either the third or fourth categories.

The light of God never fails!

You must know that the light of God never fails. When it is directed into a situation or condition, it always has an effect. What is important is the focus and purity of the decrees or prayers that direct that light. If you could see the light as some can, you would see it being released and adjusted according to the will of God.

The equation? So much of what happens is, in a sense, mathematical. Karma is considered and weighed, sometimes on an individual scale and sometimes on a national or planetary scale. The light may be allowed to lessen or ease a situation but not entirely change it because the lifestream must work through the particular karma in order to learn an important lesson. Otherwise the light would be allowed to reverse the condition completely.

My death was a good example. On one hand, all of the decrees and prayers given by my family and friends did not keep me alive; on the other hand, my transition, as I have described it to you, was so easy. I was so clear about all that I was encountering due to the decrees given on my behalf. I was also spared having my condition drag on any longer than it did.

At other times, for instance, people may get into an accident and the perfect individual is at the scene to assist them or even to save them. All of this is the light of God. It never fails to do what the law can allow, given the karmic equation of the particular situation.

The saddest thing is to watch people who feel that God has abandoned them. God never abandons anyone, but many abandon God due to their bitterness and hurt. People want God to stay with them through every wrong choice they make, but when their karma comes due, they blame God.

We are given the chance to create our own debit and credit sheet. The difficulty is that debts come due. Every right action that we have taken helps us and may give us some mercy, but it cannot erase the whole debt. As you will note when you read the lives of the saints, even they were not spared some very difficult ordeals. Some of their difficulties, of course, were due to their willingness to bear planetary karma so that the planet might be saved and thus move forward. But until they balanced their personal karma, they continued to face hard situations. The lesson is in the light, faith and understanding with which they triumph over their hard times.

Look deep into your soul and ask yourself: Is there anything that I am blaming God for? What will it take for me to let go of this? The more you become one with the light, the more you will understand that it never fails.

CHAPTER SIX

The Magic Elixir

The power of the violet flame

If I discovered the violet flame and was thinking as an entrepreneur, it would be the equivalent of finding a marketable fountain of youth.

The violet flame is a multifaceted flame. If it were a product, we would be saying: "Get seven for the price of one. Seven unique uses for one purchase price—mercy, forgiveness, freedom, opportunity, alchemy, diplomacy and transmutation."

I think that if any aspect of the violet flame is neglected, it is the flame of opportunity which Portia, Saint Germain's twin flame, sponsors. Many lightbearers pray daily for new, better or different jobs, but they rarely think to invoke the flame of opportunity, which can help open the door to new options.

As you know, I did not understand the violet flame while I was in embodiment. This is one of my greatest regrets as I look back on my life. The violet flame is perhaps the greatest dispensation you have been given; yet many students of the ascended masters take it for granted.

At its most powerful, its greatest gift is that it can change atoms and electrons. This is how Saint Germain was able to transform hand-cut stones into gem quality and to remove flaws from diamonds in his European appearance as the Comte de Saint Germain.

Jesus used the violet flame in many of his miracles. Purple has been thought to be both a royal and a holy color; adepts of all ages have known of its power. The gifts of the Holy Spirit are tied to this flame. If you have an illness, the violet flame can reverse the entire condition, unless the illness is a karmic necessity for your spiritual evolution.

The masters believe in seeking the consultation of a doctor. It may be a person's karma to go through treatment, including surgery and medication. The violet flame can assist in the speed of recovery and the success of any procedure.

Psychological therapy helps people to understand what is behind some of their behaviors, fears, moods or anger. The violet flame, then, helps to dissolve the cause and core of these behaviors.

We are accountable to wrestle with our emotions and to come into harmony concerning the events and choices of this lifetime. If we do this, God in His infinite mercy will help us transmute patterns from past lives that we do not remember or understand in our outer consciousness. Any condition that troubles a person, whether it is political, financial, medical or psychological, will always receive benefit when we send violet flame into its cause and core.

The violet flame is the foundation for the new age. <u>We will enter this age successfully only to the degree that we comprehend and utilize this flame.</u>

I am so pleased to serve with Saint Germain, but having been on earth so recently, I wonder if he is not too generous with his energy and light on your behalf. He is like a loving, concerned father who always sees the immaculate concept, or purest identity, of his children. He knows what the Christhood of even a small number can accomplish. Please do not let him down.

All that seems so real (I know it did to me)——the opinions of others, the recognition of others, worldly success and comfort——is worth nothing here. You are measured by your heart and the degree to which you have advanced in compassion, wisdom and the use of God's power.

This does not mean that certain things are wrong. The masters honor beauty and lovely surroundings, and you are meant to fulfill your dharma, or divine plan, in the earth plane. But it is when the material starts to overtake the spiritual that the soul moves into jeopardy. The fallen angels are masters of subtlety in tempting us with the things of this world. They get you not with the obvious but with the subtlest of compromises, and then they expand the wedge, inch by inch.

It is not helpful or healthy to live with a sense of burden or unworthiness. The masters rejoice at every step you take in the right direction, and they allow for your need to follow certain detours. But they weep to see how hard it has become for those on earth to internalize and live the way of the ascended masters. Pray for the violet flame to lift and dissolve all illusion upon the lightbearers, all false sense of reality.

The way of the masters is never fanatic, never extreme. I never experienced such balance and joy in my entire lifetime on earth as I experience here. The violet flame is truly the key to penetrating through the mire of what burdens you.

When I tell you about all that the violet flame can accomplish, it is important to remember that you must give violet flame decrees from the heart, with visualization and oneness with the decree, in order for change to occur. The more you genuinely understand alchemy, the more effective you will be.[12]

The violet flame is the magic elixir of this age. It can be used to repair damage to the environment and to clean the water supply. Water corresponds to the Mother and the emotional body. It is in great jeopardy on a planetary scale. Anything that you can do on behalf of our water systems will not be a minute too soon.

People have been harsh on Mother Earth. The elementals or nature spirits are literally bowed down by neglect and abuse. The elementals are begging for more violet flame.

You must not hesitate to use the violet flame in every room that you enter and in every conversation that you have. You can give a call such as, "In the name of the Presence of God and my own Christ Self, I ask for the violet flame to clear anything between this individual and me that could interfere with my talking with him this day."

You know what a freshly cleaned room feels like. Or a

newly painted room. Well, the violet flame can give this feeling to a hotel room, office, home or hospital room.

When I arrived at this retreat, I received violet flame baths to help release me from any sense of connection to my earthly body and my tie to the earth. It felt like a total acceleration of my being. The violet flame is the cosmic eraser, the cosmic cleanser, the cosmic regenerator.

Violet is the color of the purified soul chakra. It is located between the base chakra and the solar plexus chakra. This chakra, then, needs the violet flame; your soul needs the violet flame to free it and help raise it to the level of the Christ.

The solar plexus is purple and gold flecked with ruby. The purple is the deep action of the violet flame, which is needed to balance the emotions and heal the psychology. Your solar plexus is the place for the anchoring of your emotional body. The more you can transmute your negative emotions, guided by the golden light of illumination, the more you will find perfect harmony. The solar plexus is purple because it needs more of the blue of protection.

When you are in Saint Germain's aura, you feel that anything can be accomplished. He, along with his beloved Portia, embodies all of the qualities that we have been discussing.

Mercy

Mercy is a quality of the violet flame. It is the pink-ray aspect of this flame. It is a God-quality to which everyone should aspire. What I notice is that people are constantly praying for mercy, but they are so much less willing to grant it to others.

We all make mistakes, and mercy is a welcome unguent. Remember the story of Jean Valjean in Les Misérables? *The bishop granted him mercy by not pressing charges when the thief stole the bishop's silverware. Instead he offered Valjean the gift of his silver candlesticks. This act of mercy touched the core of Jean Valjean's being. From then on he wanted to live with honor and givingness towards life.*

You do not want to miss the Jean Valjeans who walk through your life. Mercy changes the giver as well as the receiver. Mercy is not sympathetic or enabling. Mercy is transformative.

Pray to Kuan Yin, the Eastern master of mercy, to tutor your soul in the flame of mercy, for truly she is the master teacher for this holy attribute.

Why hasn't the violet flame been revealed during near-death experiences?

It is most common that people are shown spiritual truths that they are familiar with on some level. The Buddhist does not see Christ during a near-death experience, and the Christian does not see Buddha.

God tends to reveal only so many truths at a time. I am now aware of how much we are not shown and how little of the truth is understood by most people. The ascended masters have been permitted to share the greatest degree of spiritual knowledge and truth of any current teaching on this planet. But even they are restricted, as people must earn and be ready for the truths they are shown. The teachings Jesus knew could have filled the world, but apparently these teachings could not all be released during the Piscean dispensation.

In general, there is a spiritual principle that the pupil must be ready before he receives certain teachings or understandings. I am a good example of this. I was exposed to the violet flame but only now do I truly understand it. I was not ready for it in my human mind, as it was out of context with what I knew spiritually. To me it was a beautiful color, and I could appreciate a very small portion of what it represented. But for the most part, I did not comprehend the importance of this flame.

If you could interview spiritual seekers around the world, you would find that a number of them have seen the violet flame even though they do not all fully know what it represents.

I have been shown a number of things that I am not permitted to share. People always think that they would like to know more, and many seek "spiritual experiences." The fact is, no matter what a person's chosen path may be, if it is a legitimate path to God, the most important principle is to internalize the teaching.

Remember that civilizations that have been given more of the truth than ours have fallen. This is why the masters focus on the heart and on psychology, along with other spiritual practices and rituals. They do not focus on siddhis (paranormal powers) or even visible miracles because in the past these have not insured the spiritual growth of the people.

If people fulfill their spiritual destinies, we will enter a cycle when more people will exhibit the gifts of the Holy Spirit. This will be allowed when the planet is in the greatest jeopardy

*and it is most critical for people to make the ultimate choice—
the path of God or the path of mammon.*

*What I now understand is that through the centuries a
small group of adepts from many different spiritual paths have
been shown and have understood far-reaching spiritual truths.
These truths, however, had to be earned and were not given to
the people at large.*

*As a soul newly arrived to the etheric realm, I kept ask-
ing, "Why don't you tell people some of these truths?" I wanted
my own church to realize many things that they were neglecting. But, like everything here, there is a geometry, a spiritual
equation. A level must be gained before a level is granted. God
does not release truth indiscriminately, and yet it is available to
all who truly seek with the purest hearts.*

Forgiveness

*I would like to talk with you about the flame of forgive-
ness, another aspect of the violet flame. Forgiveness is more critical than most people realize. It unlocks doors to your Christ
evolution, and the lack of it closes doors to spiritual advance-
ment. When you understand how elegant the cosmic justice system is, you realize that all do and will account for their deeds.*

*Ours is to forgive and not to judge. When you forgive,
you are forgiving the soul of another so you don't hold back
that one's growth or your own. You are not condoning the
action. If you cannot forgive, you must realize that you are
creating a point of vulnerability in your own psychology and
you should pray fervently for a change of heart. Doing the
forgiveness decree daily will help you have a momentum of*

forgiveness in your aura, should you encounter a particularly difficult situation.

The decree my husband gives to the violet flame of forgiveness goes like this:

> I AM forgiveness acting here,
> Casting out all doubt and fear,
> Setting men forever free
> With wings of cosmic victory.
> I AM calling in full power
> For forgiveness every hour;
> To all life in every place
> I flood forth forgiving grace.[13]

On retribution

Retribution is a necessary part of the spiritual path. [It is a karmic law that] if you have taken something from another person, you should replace it. If you have been unkind to someone, you should look for a way to shower kindness on that person. If you have taken life through abortion, you should look for ways to serve and sponsor life and to work against that which you once embraced. This is true of drugs also. If you once promoted drugs to others or acted as a dealer, then it is critical that you spend time working against the use of drugs.

Retribution means that you have understood and come to terms with your wrong choice of the use of God's energy and that you now want to atone for this. The best way to do this, when possible, is to do the opposite of what you have done that you know was wrong.

> *I am giving this teaching because, although you must put all of your misdeeds into the fire of transmutation and forgiveness, the completing of the circle is to look for tangible actions that can allow you to serve life where you have in some way harmed it.*
>
> *Almost worse than the negative act is the self-justification that can block you from atonement and retribution. The ultimate goal is to be free of these burdens, which do not come from the Real Self, and to be whole before your God.*

The editors questioned my husband's use of the word *retribution* in this teaching and felt he really meant *restitution*. However, when we asked him about his intent, he said that retribution, though it implies punishment, is not to be misunderstood. There is a karmic repayment that is required, and this restorative action or "tribute" would not be necessary if there had not been the "wrong" or incorrect action in the first place. He explained that, although the repayment is given in the spirit of understanding and repentance, it is nevertheless, in the end, a form of cosmic punishment that a portion of time or energy or abundance must now be given that wouldn't ordinarily be required of that soul. He said that it is not just a nice or noble thing to do, but a necessary step in the clearing of the record and the healing of the soul. He also told us that, for healing to occur, the repayment should not have a forced sense in the heart of the person who has committed the offense. The soul needs mercy and forgiveness, but it cannot evolve if it does not experience a consequence in the form of repayment for wrongful actions, which is both retribution and restitution.

The purpose and meaning of the seventh day of the week

In today's world, people have compartmentalized God in their lives. Many treat their religion almost as if it were a hobby they practice when convenient or like a sport they play on a regular schedule. And for others, God is invoked only in times of extreme crisis.

God is the pure energy of life. God is in everything. When we remove God from our lives and the planet, the only end result possible is deterioration. God was never intended to be a drawer in a large bureau of choices. God was meant to be the foundation and framework for everything. We have lost our reverence for life in one another and in the environment.

There was a purpose for the seventh day being consecrated as a day of re-creation in God. It was meant to remind us of our origin in God and to give us strength and faith to pass through the rest of the week. It was intended to be a time for the spiritual community and the family to be together. Now, for convenience sake, many businesses are open on the seventh day. Materialism over spirituality. The price being paid is enormous.

When you reach this side, you see everything for what it is and you wonder why you did not challenge more things when you were on earth.

The major question of the ascended hosts is "What will it take to wake people up?"

CHAPTER SEVEN

Meeting the Masters

What can you tell us about the teachings of Jesus?

Students of the ascended masters have been given the most profound teachings on Christianity since Christ was in embodiment.

The dispensation of Jesus and the true purpose of his mission have not been fully understood within the Christian world. He longs for lightbearers to be given the full truth, yet he knows that his teachings have, in many cases, been so altered that people would not recognize the truth and would defend what the wolves in sheep's clothing have put forward.

Jesus is astounded that so many denominations now exist, each explaining and interpreting his teachings in a different manner. His deepest sadness is that he has been so isolated in the minds of his followers. It does not seem logical to him that people accept a picture of heaven that involves mostly God, Jesus and the Holy Spirit. What he longs for Christians to understand is that it is not he but the Christ which he embodied that is indeed the open door to heaven.

His mission was magnificent—that of showing mankind their true identity in God. He was to be the wayshower. And his message was, "Let this mind be in you, which was also in Christ Jesus." (Phil. 2:5)

People hear this and yet do not comprehend it. We are meant to become the Christ. This does not mean in any way that we have come in with Jesus' attainment or with his mission or with his place before God. It does mean that there is a much higher purpose to life than most people comprehend.

This implies that we have a greater accountability for our actions. It presumes a cleansing of our temples spiritually, emotionally, mentally and physically. It means that though we may sin, our true identity is in God and not as "the sinner." Most people identify so much with their human self that they have become totally separated from their spiritual identity.

Have you seen Jesus?

Yes, I have seen Jesus, and he is everything and more than anyone on earth can imagine. He works tirelessly on behalf of this planet. He even spoke with me, as one so recently embodied, concerning my thoughts about the limitations and misunderstandings placed on his teachings.

He is touched by every true devotee, and yet he is so saddened that these souls have been denied the truth. He is indeed there when two or more gather in his name. As we come to the close of this two-thousand-year cycle since he walked the earth, he is determined that people have the chance to know the totality of his teaching.

In all that I am saying I do not want to neglect mentioning those Christians who have internalized the teachings and live in imitation of Christ. There are also a number who speak by the gift of the Holy Spirit and exhibit many of the gifts. These souls live with a spiritual fervor and joy that is of God. This is not true, however, of the majority.

A number of Christians keep switching churches, hoping to find the right minister. Their souls sense that there is more, but they have not found what they are looking for.

The minister is meant to be the spiritual teacher of his or her flock. It is a calling of God. If the minister is an empty vessel or spiritually bankrupt, he or she cannot bring the fruits of the teaching to the congregation. God cannot use such a vehicle to inspire or transform souls. Thus many dear souls go hungry and try to be satisfied by human kindness within the church community.

This is not Jesus' desire for his flock. He literally weeps at moments as he surveys the Church in total. He also weeps for those in other religions. In so many cases, the light that should be present and tangible in the house of God—whether temple, mosque, synagogue or church—has grown dim. The masters are attempting in every way to wake up the children and sons and daughters of God before it is too late.

The Sacred Heart

The Sacred Heart of Jesus is meant to be central to Christianity. The Sacred Heart is the vessel that contains the

*light essence of Christ. In the ritual of communion, we cele-
brate the body and blood of Christ.*

*In physical terms, the heart is the pump for the blood. In
spiritual terms, the heart is the pump for the pure love and
light of Christ. We are meant to seek oneness with his heart.
Our hearts are meant to burn with the all-consuming fire that
Saint John of the Cross describes.*

*The Bible tells us to take care of our hearts. This teach-
ing can be understood on several levels. One is the feeling level.
If the heart is not pure and centered, we can create hardness of
heart or a weakness of heart. Everything we do ultimately
affects the heart—diet, exercise, angry or kind words, love or
hate, selfishness or givingness, stress or harmony. The heart
physically and spiritually reflects our choice of actions.*

*You should ask yourself: What have I fed my heart this
day? How have I tended the flame of my heart this day?*

Jesus' teachings on reincarnation

*Jesus was the Messiah. He brought us the message of
salvation for our souls. This message has been tampered with
and changed by many hands through the ages. This should not
surprise you when, even as I speak, scholars are coming up
with new versions of the Bible.*

*Our greatest loss has been Jesus' teaching on reincarna-
tion. This teaching gives us the understanding that the true
purpose of life is to become one with the Higher Self, or Christ
Self, and that for most souls this takes many lifetimes to
achieve. Does the teaching on reincarnation really contradict
Jesus' teachings? How could the disciples have asked Jesus if the*

blind man was born blind due to his sins or the sins of his parents (John 9:2) if they didn't understand the law of karma and reincarnation?

Many Christians misunderstand Jesus' teachings and think that it is blasphemous to say that each of us can become the Christ. What they do not see is that this takes a spiritual dedication that few seek or even know to seek.

We are not declaring the human self as having any oneness with the Christ. Putting on one's Christhood is a day-by-day, often century-by-century choice made by the soul to purify and to merge with the light of the Christ. This takes sacrifice, surrender and discipline. It takes charity, wisdom and humility. It takes all that Jesus exemplified. Individual Christhood is not the deification of the human; it is the acknowledgment of the divine within us.

When you contemplate divine justice, does it really make sense that we only have one chance, one lifetime, to both accept Christ and to make it to heaven or else be condemned? Look at the seeming inequities to which people are born—some to riches and others to poverty; some to love and kindness and others to abuse or indifference; some to health and others to illness. And the list goes on.

Similarly, only some are born Christian while others are born Hindu, Buddhist, Muslim, Jew, Zoroastrian, and so on. Would God have set up a system where only Christians make it back to heaven?

In my most recent embodiment I saw isolated towns in the backcountry of Turkey bordering Russia. There were people whose families had been Muslim for centuries, and

Christian missionaries had not reached all of these villages. Does this mean that the people who lived there deserved a lesser place with God?

The truth is that when these souls pass from the screen of life, they are given the opportunity to know of the Christ Self and to accept it. A righteous soul will always accept the Christ. And thus Jesus' words are fulfilled: "I am the way, the truth and the life: no man cometh unto the Father, but by me." (John 14:6) The Christ is the open door and the way to God.

Jesus told us that he could have been saved by legions of angels had he chosen to call on them. Yet until recently, many have ignored or given little importance to the angelic realm. Similarly, Mother Mary has appeared to numerous souls as an intercessor between them and Jesus. Yet few but the Catholics understand her role.

The Bible speaks of Elijah come again. (Matt. 17:12) Where was Elijah staying before he came again?[14]

Yes, there are saints in heaven who are the ascended hosts. They have all merged with the Christ, and they all revere Jesus for the extraordinary mission he took on.

If you find it hard to believe that people might tamper with the teachings of Jesus, do some historical research. Why do you think the Book of Revelation includes the admonishment that anyone tampering with it would be stricken from the Book of Life? Because there needed to be one teaching that would remain pure. Look at how different it is from anything else in the Bible. Notice the symbology. Few have known how to interpret it, so many ignore this book; yet it contains many of the keys to the age we are in.

We also find that upon the death of saints from both East and West there has been dissension among their disciples over the true import of their teachings. Then two or more orders or sects have sometimes arisen from what was the one teaching of the saint or guru, and new interpretations of the master's teachings have emerged.

There are still books that remain on earth that have not been discovered. Others have been found but not translated, and yet others are known but have been kept from the public. All of these would support what I am telling you and what the Messenger has taught.[15]

Why do people feel that it lessens the role of Jesus if we all have an inheritance in God to choose to become the Christ? Jesus is still the exemplar. He came to share this path of his Christhood with us. We have denied him the fulfillment of his teaching. In doing this, we have in many ways protected our lesser selves. To acknowledge his true teachings would mean a revolution in light, spiritual direction and purpose on this planet.

Today so many churches want to make the human feel comfortable. But the equation is not one of human entertainment and comfortability. The equation has always been one of light. When people meet the Mother Teresas of this world, they know that they are in the presence of unconditional love and utter humility, and they feel light or radiance in this presence.

Mother Teresa has met the equation of light because she serves the Christ in all. She may not understand all I have shared with you, but she does understand the principle of seeing the Christ in all that she encounters. In so doing, she is holding the immaculate concept for each one's true identity in God.

Jesus' role in saving the planet

I wish to tell you more about Jesus' role in the saving of this planet. Do you realize the significance of this 2,000-year cycle? He has stood by the lightbearers for centuries, waiting to see if we would ever wake up to the truth of his teachings. He has held a balance for us that he is no longer allowed to carry in the same way.

God is a generous father. But the moment comes when we must either rise to reflect all that we have been given or fall in our unwillingness to see and to live the truth. We must now carry more of our own burdens, and people are finding this difficult. The answers are all in Christ's teachings, but we must become them.

Jesus would be willing to continue to carry our burdens, but this is no longer lawful for him. God will not permit it. It would only enable us to continue on as we have been. This is a time for people to wake up, to grow up spiritually, so to speak. We have been given all that we need; now we must do the hard work.

When your burden is indeed light, you will be able to fulfill your destiny. We owe this to Jesus and must not fail him.

On Gautama Buddha

I wish to speak about the Buddhic path. As you know, I always liked Gautama Buddha and appreciated his presence in the statue in our home. I did not, however, begin to understand the Buddhic way.

Most Christians never delve into the Eastern teachings. They believe that God can only permit salvation through a belief in Jesus Christ. Though this is true in a way, what they don't allow for is the timing by which a devout, God-obedient soul can be introduced to Christ. Many dear souls of all persuasions accept Christ as they make their transition and see that it is the Christ Self that is the doorway to God.

Buddha preceded the dispensation of Christianity. How can any God-fearing person study his life and not see that he was sent on a mission from God? Few of his teachings contradict our Christian beliefs. His way of meditation would be very helpful to any soul trying to reduce stress and grow in communion with God. His wisdom is unparalleled. His teachings on desire, the Four Noble Truths and his Eightfold Path are timeless.

Buddhism has become perverted in many temples, but in those cases where the true teachings remain, it represents one of the legitimate paths to God.

Buddha has been to our retreat on two separate occasions. The quality of peace that he brings with him, along with the illumination, is almost blinding.

So much opposes his flame on earth. People cry out for peace, but they live outside the boundaries of peace in both their inner and outer lives. If more people had an inner harmony and peace, the planet would move in that direction.

What keeps you from peace? Meditate on this. Wrestle with it. Bind the forces of anti-peace!

People want illumination but they do not recognize it when they are in its presence. Wisdom is not old-fashioned. It is, however, in short supply. People have chosen to honor intellect over wisdom—even in many of the seminaries, synagogues and temples of this planet.

The higher up you go in the world's educational system, the more you find intellect and human intelligence and the less you find wisdom. This need not be. This should not be. Pray for our universities to become temples of wisdom.

We do not elect wise leaders, for we have lost sight of the true wisdom of leadership. People tend to think that it is a dream, a false hope, a fairy tale to want a leader who is exemplary, who has integrity, wisdom, honor and compassion. This is because we are losing sight of what is possible and right. We have become cynical. The maya is all around and grows denser.

We must demand a new day for planet earth. We must invoke God-solutions to every problem we face. The angels are awaiting assignments. We must call for God-government on this planet.

Mark Prophet

The ascended masters approached Mark L. Prophet to be trained as their Messenger in 1936 when he was 17 years old. From 1952 to 1958, he published a series of letters by the ascended master El Morya, who, as the Master M., had helped to found the Theosophical Society in his last embodiment. In 1958, El Morya directed Mark to go to Washington, D.C. to found The Summit Lighthouse in order to publish the teachings of the ascended masters and to begin delivering live dictations from them. Seven ascended masters gave the founding dictations of The Summit Lighthouse through Mark in the presence of the original board members on August 7, 1958, in Philadelphia. In 1961, his twin flame, Elizabeth, joined him, and she began to be trained for messengership as well. She took over as Messenger when Mark passed away and made his ascension in 1973.[16]

Have you met the Messenger, Mark Prophet?

There is so much to say about Mark Prophet, now called the ascended master Lanello. He truly has the magnanimous heart and is known for this quality in the etheric realm. It is an attribute we would all do well to seek. Each person can ask himself, How magnanimous is my heart?

I have been able to talk with him on several occasions, as he has taken a great interest in this dispensation and the opportunity that I have been given to share some of what I have learned. I am struck by his wisdom and humility, and I enjoy his humor.

He has told me that few people realize how challenging and almost severe the training was for his wife and divine counterpart, Elizabeth, to enter the role of Messenger. He watches people leave the path, or stay with anger or hurt, because of disciplines and demands that are far simpler than she endured. He mentioned that it was one of his greatest challenges not to hold back or temper in any manner the tests that she needed to receive in order to fulfill her spiritual destiny.

He wants you to know that his twin flame, or twin soul, has now been thrust into a similar role. She realizes what a soul needs to progress, but the very nature of the test is for the

*soul not to see why it needs what it is receiving. This is the trial
by fire. These tests can be brief but they can also last for years.
The lesson is to stay tethered to the path in faith and to continue on in service and in love.*

*I recommend that if you will study Lanello's last
embodiment, you will learn much about faith, adherence to the
will of God, overcoming every obstacle, and also about joy.*

We asked the following question because we knew that my
husband was embodied with Saint Francis as a brother in his order.
This saint later embodied as the Master K.H. who, along with
El Morya, founded the Theosophical Society. His ascended name
is Kuthumi, and he serves on the yellow ray of illumination.[17]

Have you seen Kuthumi?

*I have not only seen him, but I have been privileged to
have several long talks with him. He is, as you know, a master of psychology. He has given several lectures to those of us
who can still make our ascension yet are not currently candi-
dates for it.*

*The purity of the love he developed as Saint Francis and
his capacity to bear the stigmata earned him great control over
the emotional body. Of our four lower bodies, the emotional
body is the one which most people have difficulty mastering. In
his mastery Saint Francis gained control over the solar plexus
and obtained the presence of Christ's peace.*

*The control over the emotions, which I certainly lacked in
my last lifetime, is gained only when your attachment to God
and to becoming the Christ is greater than any of your desires
for the world. As I look down I see that few people have this*

level of commitment to the path. Many love the path and want to grow spiritually, but their attachments to the world are still taking precedence over their union with Christ.

In order to gain control of the solar plexus and emotional body, one must be truly willing to face one's own psychology and master it down to the last erg. Kuthumi desires to release a level of teaching in this area that surpasses anything that we have yet learned about psychology. I feel helped and freed in a way that I could never have imagined by the new understanding he has offered me.

These teachings could alter the field of psychology in substantial ways, but the lightbearers have not yet earned the dispensations for them to be released. Perhaps you could put this in your decrees and your prayers.

On what day will you declare spiritual warfare on the momentums that are holding you back? On what day will you achieve the humility to seek any help that you may need, whether spiritual or psychological counseling, or increased work at the altar? For each the answer is different, but the test is not to deceive yourself concerning your own needs.

There is a pall of depression over the planet. It must be addressed. It is weighing down the lightbearers and all who are sensitive. Decree for its dissolution. Strive to stay above it in the spirit of joy.

In Kuthumi's presence the dents and rents in my psychology became so obvious, as did the path to the healing of my psychology once and for all. I wish this gift for all lightbearers, as it is the path to your freedom. In his presence there is nothing to hide behind; in the world there is much to hide behind.

Sometimes unknowingly, and other times consciously, we deny, blame, hide, resent and lie in order to avoid looking at our psychology. It follows us through lifetimes until one day we declare, "Thus far and no farther! I wish the peace of Christ to be within me, and his harmony and love. I am ready to face all that has kept me from my Real Self." And when you really mean this, the hand of Kuthumi will join your own.

Do not neglect the healing of your psychology in relation to the Father/Mother God. We tend to focus on our human relationships, but what is the nature of your relationship to God? For what do you blame God? For what are you angry at God? For what do you distance yourself from God? When do you let God into your life and when do you omit God? How do you see and understand the Father/Mother God? This is a key to your healing.

On "The Prayer of Saint Francis"

I think that what is hardest about being on this side is watching the many ways in which people are blinded by their own karma and their false sense of reality. So many people pursue activities that will count for neither good nor bad in the etheric realm. I say this with the total awareness of my recent time on earth and my own propensities to some of the same activities and illusions. So, as you select your activities, ask yourself, Is this how Jesus would have spent his time?

I have a deep desire to reach out and save every lightbearer that I can and to help them to see what I did not always see myself. And yet it is only lawful for me to share certain truths. The rest either need to be earned or cannot be revealed at this time.

Consider praying to be shown what blocks you from see-ing and comprehending the maximum amount of the ascended masters' teachings.

There are many keys and clues in things that I have shared with you, if you will allow yourself to ponder them. Many of the most profound teachings are quite simple and yet demand that we fully challenge all that is unreal within us. Much of what you need to aspire to is contained in "The Prayer of Saint Francis," which I carried in my wallet until the time of my passing.

There are two levels on which you can interpret this prayer. On one level, if you become or embody all that is in this prayer, you will be like an antidote to all that oppresses eternal life. Your presence will be similar to a bolt of healing light to all that you encounter. They will experience peace, love, pardon, faith, hope, light and joy in their interactions with you. They will long to know the source of this light, and you will be able to tutor their souls.

The other level on which you can study this prayer is a very personal one in which you study each line, looking honestly at where you stand on the attributes being mentioned. You must examine what in you finds it hard to exemplify what is being stated.

Lord, make me an instrument of thy peace.

To have true peace, which is the Christ Presence, is to radiate and embody all that is included in this prayer. If you are to be an instrument of peace, then you must face all that blocks harmony within you.

Where there is hatred let me sow love;

If you are to be an instrument of love, you must examine all that is anti-love within you.

Where there is injury, pardon;

When you are hurt you must seek to pardon, for through pardoning you can keep harmony and sustain love.

Where there is doubt, faith;

When you have doubt, seek to face the core of your doubts. Faith is greater than doubt if you truly embrace it. Ask yourself, Why do I give such power to this particular doubt? Why do I allow it to be greater than my faith?

Where there is despair, hope;

When you are in a state of despair, remember hope. Despair eclipses the True Self. Hope allows you to proceed.

Where there is darkness, light;

At your darkest moments, attempt to remember the light. Light is the alchemical key.

And where there is sadness, joy.

When you are sad, bind all anti-joy energies in your aura or that are being sent against you. Sadness attracts discarnate entities or earthbound spirits of anti-joy and heavy or burdensome energies. Violet flame decrees or music can be very helpful when you are sad.

O Divine Master, grant that I may not so much seek to be consoled as to console; to be understood as to understand;

When you are burdened, one of the very best remedies is to console another person and try to understand the burdens or *pain that he or she is experiencing. It is not that you ignore your own pain. It is critical to face it, and I have talked a great deal about the importance of resolving, through counseling, the blocks in your own psyche. But dwelling in your own pain day in and day out only increases your burden. It is truly a privilege of the path to be of service to others. Do not neglect this sacred calling.*

To be loved as to love.

When you give love unselfishly, more love comes to you. It is the spiritual law.

For it is in giving that we receive,

When you give unselfishly to others, you will receive. It is a spiritual law.

It is in pardoning that we are pardoned,

When you pardon and show mercy to others, more mercy will come to you. It is the spiritual law.

And it is in dying that we are born to eternal life.

And in dying—dying to all that is unreal, and living the words of this prayer which are real—you are born to eternal life.

I knew Saint Francis. His life and this prayer were one. The healing peace of his presence made an indelible mark on my soul, which I have carried through the centuries.

CHAPTER EIGHT

Karma and Reincarnation: Lessons of Lifetimes

Balancing karma

Have you noticed how often the masters have advised you to balance your karma while you are in embodiment rather than waiting until you are on the other side? I cannot emphasize enough how important it is for you to internalize this message. While you are in embodiment there are literally nonstop opportunities to transmute karma. You are constantly placed in situations with people you need to be with. When specific cycles are completed, you often move on to a new group, job or neighborhood.

It was not a fluke that I selected a job that allowed me

to live in many different locations in this country and around the world. I had both ancient and recent karma in each of the areas where we lived. Many of the situations, like those in which a boss or a co-worker may have appeared to be less capable than I was, had a direct correlation to what I needed to learn. I had had many lifetimes in leadership. I had a tendency to take over and dominate, not letting others contribute to the level of which they were capable. I was kind, but limited others' growth without realizing it. I required an embodiment in which I could lead and have impact, but where I was still not the primary leader or decision-maker. I needed to experience having a clear solution or excellent idea, without having the power to implement it unless my boss gave me the opportunity or had the ability to share my vision. The choices I made in turning down some apparently excellent job opportunities through the years were decidedly correct for what I most needed to learn and transmute.

I did not leave this lifetime with any grudges or resentments; for this I am more grateful than I can express. You are far freer when you are not holding on to a particular situation or person due to a lack of resolution or harmony.

You can work out many things here in the etheric—but not all. Some require re-embodiment. Others require tremendous service and decree work. It is an interesting equation. More is asked of you here than would be asked on earth. Here you see clearly what you need to do, while in embodiment your vision is often dim or unclear. You might see what is really cosmic opportunity as a burden, and you neglect to take the necessary steps or to learn the lessons that the situation was meant

*to provide for you. On this side you pay, you might say,
for neglecting the opportunity—and you still have to overcome
or transmute the karma of the situation. Some things can be
re-created on this side and others cannot; the price for these is
re-embodiment.*

*From the etheric we witness numerous situations where
people are angry or resentful of their circumstances. They never
stop to realize that their very salvation lies in overcoming with
love that which has been set before them.*

The early years of our marriage were very interesting for our
family as we moved around the world in the service of our country. At that time none of us had any outer understanding of
karma, and I was often upset about some of the apparently unfair
things that happened to my husband. He might have been
annoyed at the time, but soon forgot about it. I often wondered
how he could do this. So, hearing the preceding story from him
has been enlightening and freeing for me.

There were times when I wanted my husband to leave the
army, such as when he was offered what appeared to be a truly wonderful opportunity in civilian life. He would think it over but would
always reject the opportunity and decide to stay in the service. Now
we can understand that something was always guiding him on an
inner level and his soul knew the path that he must follow.

While in the army, my husband was sent to Turkey for a
year, from April 1963 to April 1964. He was with a small group
of Americans in Erzurum, a town high in the mountains near the
Russian border. This group served as advisers to the Turkish army
in that area. My husband was the administrative officer and was in

charge of the hotel where they lived. He supervised all the Turkish help there. He planned all of their parties and even wrote to me for recipes, which he taught the Turkish cooks how to make. So in various ways he had a lot of contact with the Turkish people.

During that year my husband wrote 150 letters to me. I recently found these and have been reading them since he died. To write to me that often, my husband had to scrape up any news he could think of, so he told me many things he wouldn't have bothered with otherwise.

The Americans entertained the Turkish army commanders a lot, and in return they received many invitations to Turkish parties. The Turkish generals spent a lot of time talking to my husband. One general always wanted to speak French with him to practice his language skills. This is not the type of relationship one would expect between a general and a much lower ranking officer. I wonder if the Turkish generals recognized my husband at a soul level and had a memory of serving with him in Turkey centuries ago when maybe he was a general and they weren't.

Additionally, the tour was hard on my husband physically, and it came at a time when it was extra hard for him to be away from his family. One day we asked him what he had learned about the spiritual purpose of his year in Turkey.

What can you tell us about your year in Turkey?

I can tell you that it was imperative that I spend time in Turkey. I owed a lot to that country from a previous embodiment. It was important that my work be excellent and that I establish good will with the Turks. I had served there many centuries ago. I had been well thought of as a general, but in the final analysis I did let my country down in several ways.

I have served in the military on a number of occasions, and I have had many high-ranking positions that I have not fulfilled with the highest dignity due to alcohol, power and women. It was critical that I have a humbler position I could fulfill with integrity and honor.

This does not mean that I did not do good work in the other lives. But the letter of the law is precise, and I had some unfortunate habits to overcome. It was critical that I have you as my helpmate in this life, for without you I could have failed once again. My desire to help others, which was truly heartfelt, had been with me for some time. It has helped to balance much that I have not done correctly.

What people find hard to understand is that in this period of time major karma has come due. People have negative momentums that sometimes follow them for lifetimes. In some cases an ancient but severe violation of the law suddenly comes due for balancing. This type of burden is the hardest to bear because there seems to be no logical reason for the current severity of the situation facing an individual.

Nothing happens without a reason. The divine justice system is elegant. There is truly no injustice in heaven. If only people could be granted the opportunity to see how many times the angels and ascended masters have tried to intervene on their behalf—how many times their suffering could have been worse—they would kneel to God in gratitude.

If I could give any advice, it would be to pray to be shown your points of vulnerability and to be willing to work on them through both decrees and psychological work.

My husband's tour of duty in Turkey came about seven years before he retired. If he had left the service earlier, he would have missed balancing that most important karma and probably wouldn't have had the opportunity to be at Saint Germain's retreat or to have this dispensation to communicate with us about what he is learning there.

We, the other members of the family, assume that we, too, must have had karma in the various places we have lived. But we didn't seem to have ties to Turkey. We were only in that country for a couple of days when we took a Mediterranean cruise some years before my husband's tour of duty there. We didn't feel the same ties there that we did when we visited other places, for instance when we were in Greece.

About a year after my husband first spoke about his time in Turkey, we again asked him to talk with us about his past lives, and he brought up his Turkish life again:

Can you tell us some more about your previous lives?

In the early sixties I was sent to a small town in the mountains of Turkey which, not long after I left, was destroyed by an earthquake. I had an opportunity to interact with tribal chiefs as well as top people in the government and military. I also reached out to the local orphanage. It was in many ways a lonely year for me, as I was separated from my family. And it was a demanding year.

When you think of all the cities and towns in the world I could have been sent to, you might wonder what the odds were that I would end up in this particular town in Turkey. But if you were to glimpse my karmic records, you would see that I had an unpaid debt to this country and, in particular, this town. As a military leader—a general, in fact—I had allowed a rather harsh destruction of this area and its people. Though I didn't conduct the assault, I did permit a person whose judgment I should not have trusted to be in command of the unit. He turned out to have a cruel streak and he did much unnecessary killing and destruction. I had grown up with this man and so had allowed myself to be deceived by his long-term friendship. As I look back I see that he encouraged momentums in me, such as overdrinking and sexual misconduct, which were destructive to my being. He was used by the fallen angels to draw me down, and I was blind to the true nature of his heart.

I was respected by most of my colleagues because I followed a code of principle in my work. Nevertheless I was accountable for entrusting power to a man who did not use power wisely or justly.

The important lesson of this lifetime is that it matters what company we keep and in what manner we keep the company. We should hold the immaculate concept for everyone. But when we appoint people to positions of responsibility or select them as our closest friends, we must pray for the discernment of God. The higher we rise in positions of leadership, the more accountability we have for the people we surround ourselves with, from whom we take advice and to whom we grant decision-making power.

The fallen ones work overtime to plant their people next to lightbearers who, due to karma and lack of discernment, can be influenced by those whom they have wrongly trusted.

No one who truly loves our souls will encourage us to do things that advance our lower natures and eclipse the Christ.

By returning to this town and serving its people in a way that was kind and just and guided by Saint Germain's diplomacy, I was able to balance my debt to the area. Many of the same souls were living there centuries later, so I actually served some of the same individuals whom this man had ruthlessly harmed.

Can you tell us more about the soul who contributed to your karma in Turkey? Were you with him in other lifetimes? Is he still in embodiment?

There are souls you keep encountering, sometimes for good karma and at other times for reasons of unresolved negative karma. There are individuals whom you encounter only in one lifetime and others who may share a portion of two lifetimes with you. And there are some whom you encounter lifetime after lifetime.

As far as I know, this individual had been with me in Turkey on several occasions before the encounter that I described. After that, we had one last embodiment together. I was able to pass my test and therefore he was no longer a figure in my subsequent lifetimes. He is, however, still in embodiment and has not to this day bent the knee. He is a fairly prominent individual in the Middle East.

The last time I encountered him was again in a military embodiment. We were officers of equal rank. He was at times charming and outgoing. On one level I was drawn to him but on another level I felt a strong sense of foreboding in his pres-

ence. I was uncertain of the origin of my feelings, but they made me cautious. As the months passed we were thrown together on a number of occasions. I discovered that he was deceiving our commander and was very adept at doing so. He was receiving bribes and giving away key information to our enemies. But I had no tangible proof to give to our commander. Knowing that it would be my word against his, I challenged this man and reported what I knew to the commander.

Although our commander was not a bad soul, he could not accept the truth of what I was saying. I was eventually reassigned and nothing was done to remove this person. I had passed my test and the commander had failed his. This is an example of how some cycles of karma end and others begin.

There are great lessons in this scenario. Corruption can be very clever. It wears many facades. It can cloak itself in seemingly friendly, articulate and charming guises. It is adept at stroking the egos of others. It is an artist of manipulation. Pray for the corrupt ones to be exposed and for them to stand naked next to their evil deeds. Pray that you will never be deceived or made vulnerable by the needs of the ego.

Were you embodied at the time of Jesus?

I was a shepherd at the time of the birth of Christ. I was not one of those who actually stood by the location where Jesus was born. I did, however, have a cousin who was led to the manger and who saw the babe shortly after he was born. An angel led him to the scene of the birth.

We were a simple people and quite devout. So when my cousin returned and shared his story with me, it had a profound *effect on my heart. As a shepherd I had many hours to myself and much time to pray. I prayed fervently for this child for many years, but I passed on long before his mission was fulfilled. I saw him on a number of occasions but not to speak with. I never doubted that he had a divine purpose and that he was most likely the Messiah.*

Many simple people throughout the ages have done more good for God than have their counterparts who appeared more learned and were more prominent before men. This was one of my best lifetimes, as I rendered a service that no one knew about, and I did it with humility and with great faith in the plans of God. I did not begrudge my station or my day-to-day life. It was one of my most peaceful lifetimes, and yet it was a life of sacrifice and scarcity in a human sense.

Have you had any embodiments with the Messenger?

She and I have lived at the same period of time on several occasions. The ones that I am most aware of relate to the Catholic Church and the military. I was her first confessor in her lifetime as Catherine of Sienna. I was also a brother in the order of Saint Francis when she was embodied as Clare. I was a soldier in a position of leadership when she was in a position of nobility. In all of these lives, I have been her supporter, although I have not risen to the spiritual level that I might have, given the saintliness of my companions.

You see, I could understand a woman being a holy nun or having a position of power in a monarchy, as I have had many lives in the Catholic Church and in the military of nations with monarchies. But I could not accept a woman as a spiritual leader. Most of my more recent lives have been lived in the Catholic Church with its patriarchy. This created a large block to my recognition of Elizabeth Prophet as the spiritual head of a church.

Despite my outer blindness, I frequently supported and helped her church because I believed strongly in freedom of religion. And I realize now that I was often taken to the retreats at night for study. This is why God's Messengers have always warned against judging others. No one can judge by outer appearances where another person is on the path.

My embodiments with Francis and Clare

I think that a very interesting life of mine was when I was in the order of Saint Francis. I joined after Francis had more fully developed his rules and his order, so I was not in on the foundation of his teachings.

I did not object to the demands of his path, as many brothers did. But I also missed the most important thing, which was to aspire to become all that Francis had achieved. What I am trying to show you is that it is possible to do all of the outer actions: I lived in poverty, I prayed, I served. But I missed the truly transformative portion of the teaching. I loved and admired Francis. I was not one who rebelled against his rules. Perhaps I more idolized him than looked at what I should become. Do not mistake my words. I did make progress, but I should have seen and internalized more.

Not only did I know Saint Francis, but also on several occasions I met Saint Clare. I tell you this because many people feel that they would be changed if only they could see *a master or if only Jesus walked among us today. The fact is that many of us lived during the time of Jesus and we are still here today. Many of us have known saints. They have gone on and we are here.*

Do not miss what you can learn from the Messenger, but beware of the subtleties of idolatry. The teachers are the wayshowers. They cannot hand you your attainment. You must earn it. They do model for you the example of what is possible, and they do offer you the spiritual tools to help you progress.

CHAPTER NINE

Dharma

DHARMA IS A HINDU CONCEPT that refers both to cosmic law and to the duty of conforming to that law or to your own nature as a manifestation of that law.[18] My husband used the term to describe the life plan each person is born with.

Fulfilling one's dharma

Many souls do not give priority to pursuing their given dharma. Dharma is what you have come to fulfill. It is what you alone can contribute in this lifetime. By finding your true dharma and fulfilling it, you help others because, in a spiritual sense, the planet benefits when individuals connect to that one chord that is theirs to play in this lifetime.

Instead, I observe individuals who choose one poorly constructed money venture after another. These are often good souls who mistakenly feel that they have found the perfect way to gain abundance even though the way may be risky, confusing and not anchored in wise economic principles. Their hope is usually to have a quick source of money to help themselves, others, their church or their favorite cause. These are lawful hopes, but they are so often not anchored in God-reality, and nowhere in the picture is the pursuance of dharma.

There will always be those who make investments that lead to great financial freedom and those who, by chance, win lotteries and contests. Most of us will not fall into these categories. Most importantly, these should not take precedence over dharma and our spiritual liberation.

There are other ways people avoid their dharma. Some simply take the first job that comes to them without effort. Others accept a secure but unfulfilling job and continue in it for years. They are miserable but indeed secure. The spiritual path does demand practicality. Bills must be paid; people must eat and have roofs over their heads. If this necessitates a period of time in a less than fulfilling job, it may be the call of the hour. In the midst of this, however, the person should continue a novena to help discover his or her true calling. It is the Father's great pleasure to show us these things, but we must ask him. And we must not lose sight of or belief in our dharma.

It is cosmic intent that we all find prosperity, but spiritual prosperity is the treasure trove from which all else can and will unfold.

Pray for discernment in your work life. Examine your motives for work and the direction in which these motives are taking you. Have you been avoiding your dharma or fulfill-

ing it? There is a peace in fulfilling it, and there is a struggle when it has not been acknowledged or discovered. Pray for God-guidance and direction in recognizing and pursuing your dharma.

Dharma is not always glamorous, nor does it necessarily place you center stage. Yours may be the mighty dharma of serving others in patience, wisdom and loving kindness. The lawful needs of the planet are far-reaching and varied, and these needs are our dharma. God does not judge us on fame or fortune but rather on whether we listen to our inner promptings and place the laws of God first.

A Good Friday message on fulfilling one's dharma and karma

In submitting himself to the crucifixion, Jesus fulfilled the hardest hour of his path on earth. Out of his sacrifice and obedience to God's plan for him, Christianity was given birth.

We must all reflect on our own willingness to fulfill the divine plan for our lifestreams. It is easy to be a follower of a true path when the going is comfortable and does not ask much of us. But are we willing to endure the hard moments? Are we willing to sacrifice that which means the most to us in order to remain true to our divine plan?

Every life has some deciding moments. Only you know how you have responded or answered when God has knocked. Many want to know what their dharma is, but not everyone is willing to do what it will take to fulfill their dharma.

And there is karma. We never escape our karma. We can transmute it, and we may receive dispensations. But one way or another it must be dealt with. Postponing the inevitable only lengthens our own path and provides more opportunities to accrue further karma.

Life is not about never making mistakes. It is about having a willingness to face and right the errors we have made.

On doing jobs that don't seem to fulfill one's dharma

No one is ever "stuck" anywhere by the dictates of God. People have free will. Part of God's desire is for them to take action with faith. Many wait for God to do everything, but the test of faith is to recognize God's prompting and to take action on behalf of what God is indicating.

God is not a spoon-feeder after a certain point on the path. We are admonished to put on the mantle of son or daughter of God. This mantle bears a price and is earned by responding to the inner promptings of the Lord. We cannot ask for divine guidance and then never listen for the answer or act on it.

Some people find change very difficult. I was such a person in a specific way. I was able to move around the world and change settings with a certain ease, but I always wanted my day-to-day life to run with the routines with which I was familiar. I chose on several occasions to keep the security of a known career over the risk of several new opportunities I was offered.

At times I reacted negatively to the teachings of the masters because it was not how everyone else thought or talked spiritually. I see now how I put false boundaries on my life and how I limited God.

The key is not to be impulsive or change for change's sake but to commune with God and listen when you do have a clear prompting. Faith demands hard decisions and at times makes the human uncomfortable. Faith equates with fearlessness.

Yes, God is practical. For one soul, taking a risk may be the way; for another, the secure job may be the right choice. The answer is always in the heart of the soul who is willing to pray and fast and seek the counsel of God.

For the most part we do create our own prisons and limitations. We are blinded by what we know and blinded in regards to what we are willing to see. Some of us are too impulsive and others are too fearful. Each person, on some level, knows where he is positioned and what the habit patterns reveal.

Do not be deceived when it appears that God is not responding; it may be you who are not responding to His signs and His clear answers.

On keeping one's spiritual post

There is a concept about which I wish to share: the spiritual office that each person holds for God. We refer to it here as the "spiritual post."

What is most important is that wherever you have chosen to live, you maintain your spiritual post. This post is like being a lamp that is guaranteed to put out a certain wattage and therefore offers light to a specific amount of space. God counts on your guaranteed light to help further His works and to hold the balance for the planet. No matter what an individual is pursuing in terms of career or study, his first calling is to this post. Unlike a lamp, your light should offer an ever-increasing wattage as you transcend yourself spiritually. But it should never go below the promised amount.

The challenges are many. First, people must understand and believe that they hold a spiritual post. They must have the attainment and discrimination to understand what change means and what it does not mean. They need to be wise in the ways of the world. I see some people losing their spiritual anchoring and succumbing to the subtle and not-so-subtle ways in which this world can dissipate light.

Pray to be shown your spiritual post and what God counts on you to do each day. If this concept does not appeal to you, then look within for what it is that you are truly seeking or perhaps what you are running from. Remember the ancient equation: From those who are given much, much is requested. (Luke 12:48) Light is meant to be honored and shared so that the work of God can manifest on this planet.

If a light burns out in a room, the room grows dimmer and, in some cases, dark. So it is with the planet and the posts that you hold.

May your light lead kindly and brightly.

CHAPTER TEN

Dealing with Personal Psychology

Personal psychology and the expansion of the heart

It is not unusual for the Messenger to tell people that their hearts have not grown in proportion to the years they have been on the path. This is why the masters have focused so much on psychology in recent years. People can seemingly do all of the right things spiritually, but if they do not face the blocks in their psychology, often they remain stuck at a certain level of the expansion of the heart.

I perceive that more men than women choose to ignore the promptings of the masters concerning working on their psychology. This is nothing to fear. It is simply another step on the way to freedom. We all have holes in our emotional bodies that need repair. We would repair a house with holes or a car with

*a hole in the engine or exhaust. Similarly, our psychology needs
to be tended to.*

*In my generation far fewer people sought psychological
help. But I can also tell you that, looking at my own psychology, the negative momentums that I had could have been lifted
by a very small expenditure of my time. I was often good at
picking up on other people's psychology but not necessarily on
my own.*

*Kuthumi is the master psychologist. You can call on him
to overshadow any therapist that is working with you. Of
course, pray beforehand to be guided to the right therapist for
you.*

*Many clues can alert you to an unresolved psychology: if
you are constantly critical of others, if you have specific fears
that will not go away, if you are regularly moody, if you are
subject to anger, if you had a challenging or dysfunctional
upbringing—all of these and other symptoms should tell you
that there are pockets of nonresolution in your psychology.
Freedom is to resolve these and move on with the path. Your
decrees can accelerate the entire process and you will most likely
experience a new level of fire in your heart.*

*You may be wondering about people like Saint John of
the Cross who understood and experienced the total power of
the heart and never dealt with a psychologist. This is true, but
times were harsher in terms of what they demanded of a spiritual aspirant. Few made the progress that he made. He, too,
faced his dweller and his psychology but in a much more difficult way than is being asked of you. The teachings that are
being released by the ascended masters come at the end of a*

millennium, just as Christ's teachings were revolutionary and started a new millennium.

One thing that you learn about the masters is that they do not waste words, and they do not sit around and chat. There is meaning behind anything and everything they say, and there is a message for everyone in their words.

In the final analysis, we each have free will to decide what we do and do not need. My prayer is that you do not blind yourself to anything that might help you to advance.

Comments about Princess Diana's tragic early death

The timetables of earth and the timetables of heaven are very different. Souls come for a time and a purpose, and then they are taken. Sometimes what appears to the human consciousness to be a tragedy is, in the divine sense, the fulfilling of the karmic equation for that particular soul.

Many lessons can be learned from Diana's life. She was not a saint, but she was indeed a lightbearer in the most challenging of circumstances. She made many mistakes, and she believed the lie of not being worthy. But her soul recognized several important truths and she did not deviate from those. She understood the power of love and compassion given freely and without judgment. She did not give from the surface, but rather from her heart. She gave at times when it hurt and where others have feared to tread. She did not do this for approval or for personal attention, but rather because she knew in her soul that it was right and somehow worthy before God. What many do not know is how often she gave when the spotlight was not on her and she had nothing to gain in the outer sense.

Some have had the arrogance to ask, "Why highlight her when other simple unknown souls do so much more?" First, how do they know the extent of what she has done and at what personal cost? Who can ever truly know this for another? Second, they do not understand the meaning of "office" on this planet. No one person is more important than another. However, some are born to position or office, or they gain their roles through marriage or their own works. Whatever the vehicle, their office becomes their testing ground.

When people have power and personal recognition, they have the opportunity to ennoble the ways of God or to ignore, or even slander, them. What they do can impact millions. Remember Jesus' analogy that it is harder for a rich man to enter the kingdom of God than it is for a camel to go through the eye of a needle. (Matt. 19:24) Diana, through her genuine good works and devotion to her own children, used a portion of her office very well.

Do not get me wrong. There were areas where Diana did not use discernment and where she did not understand the highest truths. She was particularly vulnerable in her relations with men and the entertainment world, and in learning to understand her own emotions. She fought a greater inner battle than many will ever know, and she faced outer forces that will only be fully revealed in due time.

The press has become unwieldy, and its power has become greater than the average person can begin to realize. We receive bias over truth, and often corruption and intrigue are highlighted over good. And yes—people are stalked by the press. But the paparazzi alone are not to blame. Perhaps Diana's death will help in some small way to challenge this media corruption and begin to right the balance. I'm not talking about the many souls in the press who are honest and who show good judgment in how they draw the line when it comes to having access to people's lives. I am talking about the business leaders and the power players in the press. They know who they are and, as with everything, no one escapes the all-seeing eye of God.

At this writing (September 1997) Princess Diana is still resting from her very sudden and unexpected transition. She will need healing and spiritual instruction for some months before her next steps can be taken.

What can you tell us about unworthiness?

Unworthiness that will not go away has usually been present for more than one lifetime. We have all performed acts that were not worthy of God or we would not still be in embodiment. Some people fear being whole. If they truly let go of their sense of unworthiness, they would have to acknowledge their wholeness in Christ.

Unworthiness creates a tremendous block between the individual and the fulfillment of his divine plan. When you hold on to the unworthiness, it is as if you are saying, "I believe my dweller (the synthetic self or carnal mind) more than my Holy Christ Self." It is also a denial of divine justice. Trust that you will be given opportunities to work out any violation of God's laws. You do not need to impose a life sentence on yourself. Ask yourself: Why am I unwilling to forgive myself and trust in divine justice?

Try repeating this mantra for several weeks: "Christ in me is worthy." Also be sure to ask God to remove all sense of unworthiness from you, within and without.

So many teachings have been given on this topic. (This would make an interesting book in itself.) The masters do not know how many more ways they can tell you that you are worthy before God.

Remember to use the violet flame and to call for the transmutation of all sense of unworthiness since your first incarnation on earth. Make this call daily. Ask the masters to show you anything in your psychology that is blocking your freedom from this momentum.

We cannot judge ourselves or others; this is God's alone to do. Wherever you are today, go forward. Do not keep staying in the past. If you cannot free yourself, seek spiritual guidance or counseling. Do not accept unworthiness. It is buying the word of Satan over the Word of God.

A good analogy is when a child breaks your trust through a disobedient act and you do not give him a way to earn back your trust. This creates despair in the child and a sense of not being understood. It often leads to more disobedience and an inner anger.

You are the parent of your soul. You are limiting your soul in the same way by essentially saying, "Nothing you do— no matter how many decrees, right actions or acts of kindness you perform—will make you worthy in my eyes." A sense of unworthiness can lead to a false idolatry of others because you are unwilling to acknowledge your own worth. My sadness, as I look at the world, is that many of the dearest souls are the ones who carry around this poison of unworthiness.

There are people who carry a sense of unworthiness for something that was not even their fault. If a child is abused, if a parent dies when a child is young, if parents argue about their children and later divorce, if one is injured and another is spared injury—these are all situations where guilt and later unworthiness may arise, even though the individual was never at fault. There may have been a karma that allowed these things to happen to the person, but the end result does not mean that the recipient was unworthy.

See yourself standing before Saint Germain and Portia (Saint Germain's twin flame) in a room with amethyst walls. Hand them your burden—your bundle of unworthiness— and watch them cast it into the violet flame once and for all. Then go forward free to serve the light.

Marriage

I would like to speak to you of marriage. Marriage is a sacrament. It is not to be taken lightly. It is God's intention that most, not all, people marry and work out their karma with their helpmate.

Marriage tends to be taken too lightly in our current times. It has been romanticized beyond what is healthy. Just as we have lost our commitment to excellence, we have lost our understanding of the commitment to bear one another's burdens.

Holding the immaculate concept for your partner, or thinking of him or her as the Christ, is not just a "nice" thing to do; it is imperative! Otherwise spouses almost trap one another in their momentums, complaining and holding a sense of each other's faults rather than their God-potential.

In this age there are more karmic debts coming due, hence more marriages that end in divorce. The problem is that many more were meant to be maintained than to end. One should pray hard and long before ending a marriage. One should never let involvement with another be the cause of the end of a marriage.

In marriage you wrestle with one another's dwellers. The "dweller-on-the-threshold" is the not-self, the self-created ego, which we create with our inordinate use of free will. If both partners' dwellers are not bound daily, this creates havoc in relationships. The fallen angels wish to find the points of vulnerability in all relationships of light. Therefore you must put the ruby ray—the full power of God's love—around your relationships daily.[19]

If people were willing to face their psychology, far fewer marriages would end. Instead, people go to no end to avoid the confrontation with the dweller that has helped to create negative patterns and momentums over aeons. Spiritual freedom and an integrated psychology are synonymous.

As we end this century, there will be a great pressure on relationships. People should guard well what they have and pray and decree for the protection of their marriages. The ending of a cycle such as this two-thousand-year cycle is far more dramatic than most comprehend.

Cataclysm can happen physically on the planet, but it can also hit individuals and families if they are not alert. The fallen ones love to ride the waves of our karma and our vulnerabilities. Guard well what God has given you, and you will have nothing to fear.

Each lifestream is different. Each marriage is unique before God. Only God can let you know the timing of things in your life. Nothing should be done with haste or without awareness of the will of God—neither the entering into marriage nor the leaving.

People feel that finding their twin flame—their divine counterpart who was conceived out of the same white-fire of God—is the answer. But really, finding your true self and resolving your psychology is the greatest gift that you can give to your twin flame.

Neglect

I would like to teach you about the crime of neglect. There is a general lack of commitment to the duties of life. If a person has a child, he or she must find the time to raise that child. The child should not be left in the exclusive care of others or be allowed to take care of himself for hours on end.

If a person accepts a job, he or she owes the employer a sense of excellence in doing the work, as well as a respect for the hours and the rules of the contract. If a person buys a house, he must care for it and keep it clean at all times and ready for the angels. If a person plants a garden, it must be cared for and nourished with water, fertilizer or whatever is needed.

There must be a sacredness and respect for each relationship we enter, each contract we sign. Today people are too caught up in what is not significant, forgetting the place of duty while neglecting to honor one's words and obligations.

Neglect breeds mediocrity and ultimately a lowering of

*consciousness, a reducing of general respect for life and one
another. Neglect leads to deterioration.*

I used the word crime *at the outset because, in a karmic
sense, neglect is a crime. It counters the way of the masters.*

*Do not promise that which you cannot fulfill. Fulfill all
that you promise. In other words, do not neglect your word.*

Constancy

*I guess what concerns me most is the ebb and flow of
consistent effort on the part of many students. One week they
are dedicated to meditating, praying, studying and facing their
psychology. The next week they are bowed down by the
demands of daily life, letting these other commitments slip.*

*The masters look for constancy. It is better to promise
less and be consistent than to promise the world at a moment
of spiritual exuberance and then fail to fulfill what you have
promised.*

*Each day is a new beginning. Do not get locked into feel-
ings of guilt for your past. Atone and move forward. The ebb-
and-flow approach leaves you vulnerable, whereas constancy
brings commitment; positive habits are reinforced and growth
is possible.*

*Examine your days. How constant are you in your
service to God and in your spiritual practice? Look for ways
to grow that are of God-reality and commit to this journey
once and for all. To do* more *than you have intended is never
a problem. It is the consistent failure to fulfill what you have
promised that makes the masters wonder about what they can
entrust you with. In the end, it is a matter of your word.*

When I was in embodiment, I was very aware that my commitment to do a novena, for instance, was a pledge that my soul had made to God. It was like a contract that I had signed, and its fulfillment was without question. I do not want to give you the impression that I did hundreds of these, for I did not. But when I did make a commitment, I always fulfilled it.

We all have cycles that demand more or less of us. Set a minimum commitment that, no matter what happens, you will not go below, and you will find that this commitment will help you through the hardest of cycles.

On the I AM Presence

I feel that the lightbearers are held back by a lack of true understanding of the I AM Presence, the Spirit-spark, the God within. God has given you a portion of His being that is your true identity, and all He asks of you in return is that you desire it above all else and reclaim your oneness with it!

If for every situation that you entered you were to call on the I AM Presence, saying something such as: "I AM Presence, go before me into this room and speak through me," or "I AM Presence, prepare this talk for me today," or "Mighty I AM Presence, I have entered a situation of danger. Take over. I shall not be moved," your whole life would be changed.

On always maintaining attunement

To be fully present at every moment means to be alert and awake. If you are fully present, then you are one with your I AM Presence and you will act and answer in a manner that is in full accordance with the will of God.

Many people are taken off guard by an unexpected phone call or an unexpected encounter with someone. In the state of surprise, they do not always speak and react on the highest level. One is more likely to say what exemplifies the Christ when he has the "I am the guard" consciousness and is in frequent communion with the I AM Presence and Holy Christ Self. The goal must not be to protect the human, but to honor the Christ in all interactions. If this were our standard, we would talk less but with much more love, wisdom and power when we did speak.

Think over your conversations of the last few days. What was your state of consciousness? Who were you concerned about and to what degree were you honoring the Christ?

Misuse of the throat chakra is rampant. Think of each word as a pearl and treat it as you would a pearl. Watch gossip, idle talk and swearing. They are all misuses of the Word and can make you vulnerable.

As you know, I did use swear words, sometimes in anger and often out of annoyance. They are both negative. Words are meant to be like cups of light. They are to be used to educate, uplift, praise, challenge evil, enlighten and for many other positive purposes.

Entities are tied to swear words. The more the habit grows, the happier the entity becomes, as it can create a home in the person's aura. Swearing in anger can destroy an entire forcefield and can put rents in the person's aura. Swearing from habit erodes, in a slower way, the power of the person's words and aura because when he swears, he is keeping the company of an entity that never wishes to ennoble, but rather to destroy. It is like willingly taking on something to destroy you no matter how good you are in other ways.

There is no true power in anger. There is power in centeredness and harmony. Therein lies the strength of the adepts.

Someone we knew of was unjustly put in prison, and we asked my husband about the situation.

On being put in prison when one does not carry the karma for it

This is a very complex question. Remember that Gandhi was imprisoned for his beliefs, as were many fighters for truth and freedom.

When an innocent person is imprisoned, and it is not the direct karma of the person to experience this, it is typically a case where a soul has volunteered to be used as a form of judgment of a corrupt system or of individuals who have been corrupt or dishonest over lifetimes. It is a sacrifice the individual makes to cause a more honest system to come forward or for the spiritual judgment of those who have knowingly compromised themselves to harm another.

Although the imprisoned one may not have a karma that calls for this, the truth is that a tremendous amount of karma is allowed to be transmuted, if he is able to pass the test that this severe treatment asks of him. That is why, through time, political and religious prisoners have emerged with a radiance and a spiritual depth that they did not have when they entered prison. God rewards those who endure and keep His name when they are being persecuted.

Persecution is part of the spiritual path. It comes in

many forms and at many different levels of intensity. The intensity of a false imprisonment is severe. But as the Bible states, blessed are ye who are "persecuted for righteousness sake," (Matt. 5:9) for great shall be your reward. As you know, Richard Wurmbrand did have this experience through his many years of imprisonment and torture.

In human terms we feel as if a portion of a person's life has been wasted. But in spiritual terms this may be one of the most important accomplishments of lifetimes.

Mistakes, sin and error

Many times, when we punish ourselves over and over internally, it is for one mistake we have made that we consider so difficult that we think we can never be forgiven. We never forgive ourselves, essentially determining that God is not capable of forgiving us. The irony is that those things for which we are genuinely repentant are forgiven long before we forgive ourselves, though this has nothing to do with the karmic recompense that may be asked of us in this life or another.

What people rarely contemplate, and are far more grievous spiritually, are patterns and momentums such as anger, gossip, swearing, selfishness and irritability for which many are never repentant. These momentums hurl energy at others and limit people and personal spiritual growth far more than one act for which the soul genuinely atones.

This was a surprise to me when I arrived here. I was thinking in the reverse. Instead I had to come face-to-face with several momentums that were not the least bit advantageous to or admirable in my character.

Pray to be shown those momentums, often lifetimes old, that are holding you back. Then pray to be liberated from them.

The story of a soul I knew

I would like to share the story of a soul whom I knew well and who recently made her transition. She entered this lifetime with specific records to overcome, but she failed to see her tests. The very momentums she came to challenge ended up dominating her life. She died having gone backward instead of forward on her journey.

She had an irrational desire to control others, particularly those closest to her. She wanted desperately to be loved and thought well of, but she controlled people to the point that she drove them away from her, or spurred their anger or dread. A deep momentum of fear fueled her desire to control. It also caused her to focus on herself and to close her heart to people she could have helped or loved. I cannot describe to you how sad this is to me. I can only pray that she will be granted another opportunity and that she will not fail again.

Her problem began in childhood. Her mother recognized these momentums but, being busy raising a number of children born fairly close together, she did not adequately discipline or challenge these patterns. She was very loving toward her children and an example of Christian faith. However, she did not provide the psychological and parental firmness this soul required. Her father didn't recognize these patterns until his daughter was much older, and then he avoided her by isolating himself from her until she was approachable. He never challenged these momentums from the level of the Christ. Basically, those close to her did not help her to face herself at a stage when it would have been much easier to alter these patterns.

It is important to note that parents are accountable to avoid either overindulging their children or neglecting them. Parents must pray to be wise tutors of their children's souls. One child may require very different handling than another. Each child has a unique personal psychology that has been formed from past experiences and is now being shaped by the present lifetime. The child's early years represent an opportunity to get a helpful start on overcoming those momentums that will attempt to rule his or her present life if they go unchecked and unchallenged. It takes profound love and patience to work with the uniqueness of every soul with whom you are entrusted. But I can tell you, it is like gold in your heavenly bank account when this is done well. Of course the child has free will, but the clarity of the messages and the parental modeling and discipline received during the first twelve years can assist the child through the rest of his or her life.

Remember that the soul I am describing was not a bad soul. She was a soul who let her dweller win over her Higher Self. She did accomplish some positive things in her work life and in several other areas, and through this she did make some good karma. She prayed, but her prayers were very often fueled by fear. Through all of this she failed to see the whole test for which she had embodied. This, for me, is the great tragedy of her life.

Do not hide from your momentums. Seek to identify them and be freed from them. The dweller loves self-justification and personal and spiritual blindness. The Higher Self loves to face anything that will free the soul from the dweller.

Which one is running your life?

I have my own accountability in the situation that I have described. As I look back on my life, I see that there were several people to whom I should have said more from a point of peace and love for their souls. I did not, and two of them in particular have had a mighty karma to face. I am not to blame for their actions, but I will never know what wise counsel might have meant or how it might have helped. I would at least know that I had acted on behalf of the Higher Self and not the human self.

It is very easy to fall into the trap of keeping a person's dweller peaceful rather than seeking to reach his Higher Self. Contemplate your own relationships. Is there anyone in your life toward whose dweller you have been catering, thus avoiding the fight for the soul?

The soul I have been describing became increasingly obsessive about controlling all of the mail she received, including junk mail, and any objects that entered her life, like plastic containers and boxes. She could not let go of anything for fear that she might need it. She would not relinquish control to anyone. She ceased to live any semblance of a normal life as her mail, papers and other articles took over her home. She sabotaged any possible help that was offered. In her early years she could maintain both meticulous order and control, but in her later years, as her health declined, she opted for control over order. Hers was an obsession fueled by fear. She suspected everyone and could not see goodness when it was right next to her.

If you find yourself judging everyone, stop and assess yourself. If you find yourself suspicious of everyone's intent, stop to look at your own intent. *If you live a life in which you have no time to help others and everything centers on you, then know that something is awry. Fear can keep you from living. Fear can blind you to the good in people. Fear can destroy your health and paralyze your feelings. Fear can usurp your dharma and become your master.*

Controlling others and seeking control over the material realm will never abate this fear. Fear is dissolved by love, and control is dissolved by humility and the love of the Higher Self. Remember that you are not truly free if you desire to control others or if you are being controlled. Likewise, you cannot know true love when you abide in fear. Seek God-control, God-love and Christ-mastery.

I did not enjoy sharing this account, but I feel that it can render a service. My prayer is that the record of this service might help the soul that I have described to move forward.

Anger

The clearing of anger from a person's being is paramount to healing, spiritual victory and personal freedom. Anger is like a parasite that lives off of and depletes a person's light source. Anger can be buried deep within the person's psyche or it can be worn on the surface. Either way, the person is vulnerable. The most difficult cases are those in which the anger started before this lifetime. Some individuals have carried a core anger for centuries, and frequently that anger is with God. Many people blame God for the circumstances of their lives. Some have failed to defend their faith at a critical juncture, yet they blame God and not themselves.

Fear and hatred usually lurk behind anger. We have become a planet where these qualities are flourishing. So much of this could be avoided if people understood the principles of personal accountability and of genuine faith, and if they had the desire to cultivate loving kindness in their hearts.

To rid yourself of this insidious energy you can pray to be shown any anger in your soul or psyche back to your first embodiment. You can ask to be shown the best method to use to rid yourself of this anger. Typically it will be a combination of therapy, spiritual work and a genuine desire to be healed. Anger cannot be ignored. It must be dealt with—or it will deal with you and others who are important to you.

It does not matter how many services you attend or how many prayers you utter. If you are leaving these moments of devotion only to lose what you have gained in prayer through angry outbursts, then you are not progressing spiritually. Anger does not want to be touched. It likes controlling the person. You must break through this force or barrier and begin to unravel its origins within you. Even if you believe that others are at fault for creating your anger, you are still the angry one and must be cleared of this energy. If you hold on to anger, you need to explore why you wish to keep company with this energy. What is it feeding? What is it hiding?

Any power that anger appears to have is empty and illusory. It may be used to manipulate people and situations, but in the end it has manipulated you into creating more karma. Anger can block the growth of your heart and its ability to love. It can also attack your physical heart. On numerous occasions the ascended masters have mentioned anger as a serious pitfall to progress. It is critical that you face any vestiges of anger that remain within you and free yourself from that bondage.

Mastering the mind

I keep asking myself why the temptations of the illusory world are so powerful, even for the sons and daughters of God. I then reflect on my own lifetimes which, by grace, we are allowed to study in order to help us see our own momentums and the areas that we need to overcome. What I notice about my last embodiment is the role that my mind played. I gave power to many thoughts and distractions that now look foolish to me. So much of life is what we grant power to. I remember thinking how wonderful it would be to own a boat, and yet, when I was finally able to own one, it meant little to me. Our thoughts have an incredible range—from desires to fears, from criticism to anger and hatred. They can also be inventive and creative, affirming and hopeful, holy and pure.

Much of what I have shared with you before has been about the heart and its central role on the path. I realize that I have said little about understanding and overcoming the per-versions of the mind, which are often triggered by emotions. There is a mastery of the mind that must be achieved along with the mastery of the heart.

It is important to contemplate the concept of maya and illusion and to truly understand the strategies of the synthetic self to keep you eternally bound to that which is not real.

One of the practices I have been working with and studying is meditation. As you can imagine, meditation has not come as easily to me as other practices and understandings have. Even in my monastic lives I garnered a great momentum in acting, planning, managing and directing, and much less in stillness and contemplation.

Meditation has many levels, as does true prayer. It is not my role or place to give teachings in this area, as I have much to learn. One practice, however, is relevant to what I am trying to say today—the practice of getting in a meditative position and attempting to clear your mind. You then watch but give no power to the thoughts that pass across the screen of your mind. What this teaches you is the level of distraction of your mental body. I think that it would help many of you to watch your thoughts, even to record them for a while, and notice the nature of your thoughts. Then try to achieve a level where these thoughts pass by as if on a movie screen while you act as observer.

We are tossed about by what we allow to control us, when in reality the Holy Christ Self, not the synthetic self, should be in control. Remember that evil is thwarted when you grant it no power. The masters have urged us to meditate on our own I AM Presence each day. They have also suggested selecting a holy affirmation or mantra to keep our minds focused on God.

Notice how often the masters have mentioned that we should resist idle conversation. This is not to discourage you from the conversation of holy friendship or family sharing. These are lawful and should be ennobling. But truly I must tell you that, as I watch, I do see how much time could be garnered for God if the idle conversation did end. This does not mean eliminating the courtesies of life or the encounters we have with people as we fulfill some of the necessary tasks of life. The spiritual evolution of a soul involves thoughts, words and deeds. You are the steward of your own being. Only <u>you</u> in holy honesty—or the ascended hosts—know how you handle these three in your life.

Seek to abide in the flame of the abundant consciousness, free from destructive thoughts and anchored in the practicality of the Mother. I promise you that much of what you seek and dream of will be yours if you seek this mastery.

Have you learned anything about hypnosis? Is it ever safe for us to use?

The difficulty with any form of hypnosis is that its use does not equate with genuine spiritual attainment. It is the programming of your brain either by someone else or by your own application. If someone else hypnotizes you, you are vulnerable to their energies or their suggestions, or to astral forces that may use you while you are in the hypnotic state. It is far safer to practice self-hypnosis. But even this is better when it is done more like an affirmation, with the name of God and the will of God included.

Many techniques can be helpful and successful when practiced by the right person with purity of motive and clarity of mind. Many practices that existed at the height of ancient civilizations that were far more advanced than our own are returning. Yet in the end these civilizations collapsed for lack of alignment with deep spiritual understanding and genuine practice. Always look at the source of what you are receiving. Humanly there are many shortcuts, but spiritually there are few.

Spiritual attainment is about transforming the four lower bodies. This implies that all bad habits and momentums can be overcome. Spiritual attainment is a path; it is not an instant formula. The timing of God is always based on an equation. A miracle may seem to happen in an instant, but a whole spiritual equation leads up to that moment. The equation is composed of attainment, karma, grace and mercy.

Have you any suggestions for people who fight such anxiety that it literally keeps them from being effective at times?

Anxiety can feel like an internal cataclysm. It can paralyze people and it can take precedence over all other events in a person's life. I cannot give just one comment or teaching on this, as its causes are myriad. Anxiety that seems overpowering and for which there is no apparent origin usually has its roots in a trauma of a previous life. Other anxieties have their roots in a crisis or trauma in this life, but the person is sometimes unaware that the origin relates to the particular event. Others have a psychological/chemical condition that causes anxiety. Finally, many anxieties are produced because people want the approval of mankind for the actions and appearance of the synthetic self. This anxiety is typically a focus on the not-self, coupled with a lack of faith in God's ability to provide for our smallest need or concern. Human success becomes more important than one's relationship to God. As the anxieties increase, they become like an electric force, which grows in intensity as more fear gets added to the coil.

This is why we must seek the resolution of our psyches.

There is a complexity to each person that cannot be handled with two-bit advice. There is a divine resolution for each lifestream who earnestly seeks wholeness.

It is very important to conquer these momentums and to be humble enough to seek help when necessary. Anxiety should never become the ruler of your days or the denier of your sleep. I was not an anxious person, but I did have some fears. I promise you that I could have been rid of all of them easily if I had dealt with my psychology.

In the Catholic Church we would turn to one another and shake hands and wish each other the peace of Christ. When you think of it, this is a beautiful offering to our fellowman and perhaps one that we should hold for all whom we encounter.

May you find this peace, for it is within each of you.

On the use of time

A helpful exercise would be to stop at the end of the day for at least one week and assess where your energy and time has gone.

How much time did you spend gossiping?
How much time did you spend being annoyed or hurt?
How much time did you spend learning?
How much time did you spend watching TV?
How much time did you spend in idle conversation?
How much time did you spend helping others?
How much time did you spend in prayer?
How much time did you spend without meaning or purpose?

How much time did you spend on your job?

Patterns will emerge and, if you are honest with your-self, an improved use of time can be established.

Remember that while people are sidetracked, they are less likely to see and to fight the forces of evil that are working over-time to destroy all that is holy and pure and of God. These forces must be dealt with and the planet must be cleared of all that is anti-life and anti-light.

Today is Thanksgiving. Is there anything that you can tell us about gratitude?

Yes. I think that most people know that it is right to thank others and that it feels good to be appreciated for some-thing you have done or for who you are. What is most over-looked, or perhaps not understood, is the sheer spiritual power of gratitude.

Thankfulness, at its highest level, is an open door to God. The grateful heart thanks God for everything that is put in its pathway—the good and the bad—because it understands that everything represents an opportunity to edify God and to grow spiritually.

Reciprocity is not adequate. Contemplate the questions: What would I be like if I lived in a state of perpetual grati-tude? and, What am I unable to be grateful for in my life?

If something very difficult happens to you and you are genuinely able to thank God for this opportunity to grow or to struggle or to experience pain, whatever the case may be, you will most likely move through or out of the situation much more quickly than if you are bitter or questioning of God's motives or in a state of self-pity.

It is spiritual blindness that keeps us from gratitude. The more a person can understand of the principle of karma and the divine justice system, the more he is able to embrace the way of gratitude.

Ingratitude can lead to a bitterness that prevents a soul with substantial spiritual attainment from moving forward on the path. If the soul dies in this state, it will be pulled down by this cancer that it has allowed to infest the body and the spirit.

CHAPTER ELEVEN

Choose Life Not Death

The ultimate ingratitude

Perhaps the most ungrateful act, and one that has resulted in a tremendous weight upon the people of the United States and other parts of the world, is the taking of life through abortion. Many dear and truly lovely souls have been deceived into believing that abortion is a "right" or lawful choice. Yes, God has given us free will. But does it seem likely that it would ever be the will of God for us to take a life?

We are accountable for our decisions. If we decide to be sexually active, we know that pregnancy is a possible consequence. Life is to be revered at all levels. The irony is that some people who honor the environment and are horrified by the destruction of planet earth and fight for many species who are in jeopardy of extinction do not see that abortion is also the destruction of life, which is holy and meant to be protected.

Perhaps the most compelling understanding comes when you are in the etheric realms and you meet souls who have been denied embodiment not once but several times due to abortion. They need the opportunity to progress, which requires that they re-embody. The soul selects her family. The soul is prepared to handle the situation no matter how difficult, and yet, if the parent decides to abort, the soul loses its opportunity.

This should not be viewed as the narrow belief of the Religious Right. This should be seen as the way of all those who understand the principle of reverence for life. Anyone who has contacted the true heart of a genuine spiritual path should know that life is holy and must be honored.

People do not deny that life begins at conception, but some do feel that they have the freedom of choice to decide whether life should proceed or not. Most abortions occur after the first signs of a heartbeat can be detected. Is this really the meaning of freedom?

I cannot adequately convey to you what a burden would be lifted from the planet if this practice were changed.

The story of an abortion

Our retreat has large movie-sized screens that are used to inform us concerning events taking place in the universe and to teach us lessons we need in order to move forward. Today we were shown the karmic records of an unmarried couple who have chosen to abort the child they have conceived.

On the screen we saw a young college girl and her

boyfriend. He is also in college but is two years older than she. The boyfriend has never considered any alternative but getting an abortion. He does not want to jeopardize his studies or his future career by having a child to care for. He has put great pressure on his girlfriend to have an abortion. What she does not know is that this is the second relationship in which this man has pressured for an abortion. She is confused and very torn. She would like to tell her family but fears that they might disown her or refuse to pay her college tuition. By deciding not to speak with her parents, she will never know what we can clearly see from our octave—that though her parents would have been surprised and disappointed, they would have supported her in having the baby and then deciding whether to keep the child or put it up for adoption.

This girl has been hurt by her boyfriend's attitude, but she loves him. Though she believes in a woman's right to choice concerning pregnancies, she is not prepared for the sense of life she feels within her. With very torn feelings, she acquiesces to his wishes and follows through with the abortion. Afterwards she feels a depression she has never experienced before.

The soul that these two were to sponsor is a lovely being who could potentially re-embody for the last time, i.e., ascend at the end of the next lifetime. But the child needs to be in a family with the father who conceived him in order to work out a very difficult karma with him. This is now the second time that this same man has caused this soul's opportunity to re-embody to be revoked. This soul feels that his progress is being thwarted and his karma with this man is intensifying. He does not know when he will have a third chance to take embodiment.

We have also witnessed scenes in which a woman insisted on having an abortion against the wishes of her boyfriend or even her husband. We have studied hundreds of cases, looking at the reasons people decide to have abortions and the karma that follows their decisions. The reasons tend to fall into a limited number of categories. Many feel that they are not ready for the responsibility of parenthood and that having a child would negatively alter their life plans. Some are afraid for their reputations and the reactions of their families. Others who are married feel they cannot handle another child. Still others feel that the planet is overpopulated and they do not wish to add to the numbers. Some are forced to have abortions by political regimes or close family members.

Many, but not all, people make this decision with a heavy heart and after much thought. Most of these decisions, in the truest analysis, are based on selfishness and self-love. They are ultimately decisions for human convenience and personal reputation. They are generally made without an understanding of reincarnation and with very little faith in God's abundance and the possibility that a solution can be found for everything when one fervently requests divine intervention.

People must be taught the laws of karma. They must be shown the importance of every soul who attempts to take embodiment. Every soul needs a body in which to work out his or her karma. The soul selects the family that will best allow her to fulfill that karma. When would-be parents decide to have an abortion, the soul they abort may have to wait a long time for another opportunity with a different family. Or she may, at a later date, be born to the same person. But this time the child may bring along an added layer of resentment or sense of conflict as a direct result of the abortion.

Abortion should never have become a liberal-versus-conservative issue. It should simply be a cosmic truth understood by all that life does begin at conception and therefore should not be destroyed. Overpopulation is one of the least of our problems, and there are God-solutions for this. But hatred, greed, lust, selfishness, pride, prejudice and ingratitude—these can destroy us.

I know that many souls deeply regret their choices regarding abortion. I can tell you that God in His infinite mercy forgives, and in His justice provides ways to atone. If you have aborted a child, do not condemn yourself or abide in a sense of unworthiness. This will do nothing for you or for God. Look instead for ways to serve and honor life.

Pray to Mother Mary for ways to solve this dilemma on our planet. She awaits you eagerly.

CHAPTER TWELVE

On Working
with Children and Youth

Helping our children experience
the kingdom of heaven

  I want you to know about the kingdom of heaven. The beauty of this realm is worth every sacrifice and every right decision to do the 'good' and the 'right.' You cannot storm heaven; you must earn your place. To be falsely pious means nothing here. I may have been outspoken and irritable at times, but I was never false to myself or others.

  It is so important to be who you are in the deepest sense. This is only possible if you face your psychology and its accompanying habit patterns and achieve the proper balance in your spiritual life. You cannot become one with your Higher Self without giving to others. In giving to others you can begin to find out who you are. This is part of the equation, not the whole equation, but part of it.

A life that is centered on the lower self can only progress so far. This is why it is so important to give young children opportunities to be of service to others. This is part of the early development of the heart.

It is also important to develop right judgment. It is a part of wisdom's flame. Children can be helped with this by having the opportunity to develop strong habits of the heart and mind. Habits of the mind involve developing a love for qualities such as excellence, thoroughness and persistence. Wise judgment is a result of good character, and good character must be fostered by parents, school, community and, of course, church. Children need opportunities to practice what they have heard about good character. They must have opportunities to be of service to their schools and communities as well as their homes.

Indulgence of children is never helpful, but respect for children helps them grow in alignment with God's principles. At its worst level, a pattern of indulgence corrupts. Similarly, a pattern of deprivation can erode the spirit. How we treat our children and the children with whom we interact is part of the way we are tested and measured.

There is a mantle of adulthood that must be worn and developed. Part of that mantle is to be a role model for every young person who touches your life. Each time we fail to wear that mantle, we accrue karma. Not everyone is meant to have children or to pursue a sacred labor that involves children, but everyone is meant to honor the child and his or her God-given potential to become the Christ.

To be here with Saint Germain surpasses everything that
I ever imagined. I want this opportunity for everyone, but it
can only happen through an honest assessment of your life and
where you are heading. You must come to desire the 'good' and
to practice these virtues in your everyday life with sincerity
and joy.

What does it mean to hold
the immaculate concept for teenagers?

There are no boundaries when you hold the immaculate
concept by holding the Christ image for another. We should, of
course, do this for our children so that they have every opportunity to reach their Christ-potential.

Many people don't realize that in day-to-day life there
must be boundaries. People's souls need to be accountable.
Children learn when there are clear consequences. Parents who
protect their children at all costs often shield them from the
lessons that would help shape their characters.

To call a young person on an illegal action does not
imply that you are against youth. Anyone who can truly discern the heart knows the difference between someone who
"judges" our youth and bears intolerance and someone who is
simply reporting the truth concerning observed behavior.

To shield anyone from his karma with human sympa-
thy is a great disservice. True discipline, which is based on love,
wisdom and power, helps to mold future disciples. Many times
parents who are unable to see the wrong their children have
done are really protecting themselves from looking within.

We should pray for the victory of our youth daily. Everyone should find some way to render a service to protect the purity and innocence of our youth.

Caritas (charity) and the Youth

I would like to talk to you today about caritas, *or holy charity. Saint Francis of Paola, Italy (1416-1567) did everything in the name of* caritas. *There was a great power in this soul who lived and breathed to be the vehicle of God's charity, or love.*

The Youth need to have opportunities to give to others. Each person should examine his life to see the level of charity that is in it. Every time we condemn or criticize or gossip about another person, we are outside the circle of charity. If you are given to frequent criticism, try to get to the cause and core of your need to do this. The way of the saints is to hold the immaculate concept.

If you have a food shelf or clothes donation area, it would be a good idea to let the Youth help with these, or even run the facilities. They could also do chores for senior citizens, and they could help in solving genuine problems within the community.

Youth need to experience the joy and meaning of giving. This will help to expand their hearts and their sense of being significant members of the community.

Working with teenagers

Teenagers are extremely judgmental of the adults around them. They are not deceived by words. They look for adults who cannot be manipulated. They look for adults with joy and balance and mastery. No matter how they behave personally and no matter what they claim to want, on a soul level teens recognize the "true" parent or the righteous adult.

The question for every parent is, What have I modeled for my child? If parents have been fanatical or hypocritical in their practices, this will have a great influence on their children. Children notice everything, and they often internalize more than we realize.

This does not mean that parents should suddenly live in fear of their every action. Like all of us, parents make mistakes. The important message, however, is to be as honest with yourself as possible.

A parent who is religious and who loves his or her child will naturally hope that their child will embrace their religion. Parents who did not find their religion until they were adults feel that their children are so fortunate to be raised with those beliefs. Of course this is true, but for the equation to be complete the parent has to understand good parenting and have respect for children. One must know how to best impart religious beliefs to a child.

Every child is unique. Some come with more natural affinity for the spiritual path, while others are swayed by the world and find it hard to have a family that adheres to a strong religious belief.

The teenage world is bombarded with unreality. If teens receive a strong foundation of reality and balance in their earlier years, they will not forget this. It is recorded in their souls. Even if they leave their church for a while, they are likely to return. *Allow them the freedom to study other faiths. Let them know that ultimately they will need to select a church, as no one else can do this for them.*

We are all tested by the call of the world. Some of us are less deceived than others. And the rare few have God-vision at all times.

The greater concern is not with the teens but with the level of good parenting they have experienced. They must see the fruits of the religion in their parents. They must also see its applicability to everyday life. They must experience the bonding of family in the greater context of faith. Parents who practice different faiths should emphasize their similarities.

What is the best approach to use in teaching teenagers about religion?

Teenagers need to feel that they have the freedom to select their spiritual path. The parents' job is to lay the spiritual foundation throughout the early years of the child's life. Children learn more about religion from how their parents live than by what they say.

Religion cannot be all do's and don'ts. It must have joy and practicality, love and kindness, discipline and responsibility. There needs to be family time and fun time for kids to remember as they look back. The rituals of families are important. Feeling listened to is equally important.

In the context of family, children learn to pray and say grace, and they attend church and Sunday school. Worship becomes an important part of family life. The children grow up seeing that faith is the foundation of their parents' lives, and they experience the many ways that praying can help in a person's daily life, as well as the life of the planet.

What should we be emphasizing in our schools?

I must start by telling you that this is not an area to which I have been assigned at this time. Since I arrived here, much of my education has been focused on spiritual principles and the science that governs the universe. I have studied the science of the spoken Word in depth. I have studied alchemy. I have spent hours studying reincarnation and the law of karma. Many of these subjects have deep implications for education, but I have not been researching our current system of education directly. However, here are some of my thoughts and observations that do relate to education.

Children must be made to believe in their God-given potentials. They must be exposed to the principle of excellence. They must see the role of learning as a necessity for their growth. They need to feel purposeful in their studies.

I am concerned that many who administer the public schools feel that an acknowledgment of God (even without mentioning a specific religion or denomination) would be harmful to our youth. It is the very power of prayer that our schools need. We have removed an important tie to God that helped protect the schools for many years.

Any way that you can find to involve parents in the education of their children is desperately needed. In this modern electronic world, the presence of ethics and deep moral values will be critical. Youth learn these things from role models and by personal opportunities to participate in "doing good."

This must be emphasized to parents and schools.

A system is flawed when one race does more poorly than another. This can be changed. This __must__ be changed. But it will have to involve parents, teacher training, communities and God.

Adopting children

We have studied the plight of abandoned children on this planet. Many have been torn from their parents due to war and persecution. Some have been left for adoption due to government policies, such as those in China, which are against the laws of God. [Editor's note: China has a policy that limits each family to only one child. Children conceived over that limit are forcibly aborted or placed in orphanages.] Some have been given up for adoption because their parents were young and ill-prepared for parenthood.

The list of reasons is long. For child and parent alike, this can be one of the most heart-wrenching moments of their lives. Even parents who have been killed long in their souls for their children to be nurtured and supported.

Remember that one of the ways a civilization is judged is based on how it has cared for its young. We are responsible for our immediate families, but we are also part of the family of God. It may not be feasible or practical for everyone who wishes to adopt a child to do so. But rendering some type of service or support to a child, whether through giving money or some other action, is a door open to most people. And always the avenue of prayer is available. Prayers can be offered on behalf of the protection of the purity and innocence of our youth.

There are adoption angels who work specifically on connecting prospective parents with the souls they are meant to minister unto through parenthood. Their work is not simple, as free will can step in at any moment and reverse a situation that was meant to occur.

The thing to remember is that you will not get a soul that is not intended for you if you pray about all aspects of the adoption, starting before you begin the process until the child is in your arms. If something doesn't work out, even at the last moment, you must be at peace if you have done the necessary spiritual work.

There are blazing souls of light waiting to be adopted. There are also souls with challenging karma and momentums. Your own karma will always be a part of the equation. The violet flame can help you transmute as much as can be allowed before you adopt, thus providing you with the privilege of sponsoring a very special soul. Adoption, though feeling more complicated on the outer, can bring you the same soul as a natural birth would have.

As they grow older, some adopted souls will eventually seek out their birth parents. Others will not or cannot, through circumstances of death or lack of records. Whatever occurs is usually a direct result of the karma of all people involved. This is not to be feared but understood as the fulfilling of the law.

It may not be necessary to physically adopt a child unless the will of God does sanction this. Rather, people must be open to sponsoring a soul financially whenever this is possible.

If you are considering how you can serve the Youth, do a novena [a series of prayers for nine days] to Mother Mary *or one of the other masters asking to be shown the clear direction for you and your spouse and/or family. Do not launch any actions impulsively, but let them be guided by the hand of God that never, never fails.*

On behalf of our youth

You cannot pray enough for the future of our youth. They must be saved. So many young people are confused, angry and lacking in hope or clear values. This should not be. The masters who sponsor youth, along with every ascended master and angel working on behalf of our youth, should be called on daily in prayer and decree.

I can imagine a group of people who would take a vow to pray and decree daily for a certain period of time for the holy innocents. Innocence is beautiful before God. Purity is the way of God, yet we have become a civilization that exposes our young to so many things that are tainted and impure at such early ages. Remember that a civilization is measured in part by the care of its young and its elders. The care that is measured is the care for their souls and their progress with God. It is possible to have a youth-oriented society in which no attention is paid to the soul and its growth.

It is a faulty concept to focus solely on the health and victory of your own family and relatives. While we must be thoughtful, loving and honorable in our relationships with those closest to us, we cannot neglect our responsibility to life itself and the greater world. We may have a karma and even a dharma with those closest to us, but we should also seek spiritual and physical ways to help solve the planet's problems.

How can we help reverse the poverty and abandonment of children worldwide?

Jesus could not have made clearer his respect for the little child. When people grow insensitive to the plight of children, they have allowed a certain hardness of heart and spiritual blindness to penetrate their beings. We cannot make a blanket statement that such misery is the karma of these children. It is, rather, that people are making karma by the ways in which they neglect the children.

Children deserve opportunity. They deserve to know human love and a caring touch in their early years. They must be told of God and the way of light and divine purpose.

Human rights should begin with the right treatment of children everywhere. Nothing defies God-solution. If all religions would unite around this issue and submit it to prayer, with specific hours or specific days dedicated to a focus on this topic, the solutions would start to come forward.

Gangs

Many dear souls are deceived by or forced into gangs. Gangs are like a cancer growing within the major cities of this nation. They must be challenged and stopped before we are unable to control them.

The cities need to be reclaimed for decent, law-abiding living. Lightbearers should support and encourage all efforts to bring safety to our streets and hope to the children.

CHAPTER THIRTEEN

Social Conditions on Planet Earth

The media

We have become a society that more often protects that which is harmful to its people than that which is best for the common good. We are so afraid to be controlled or limited in any way that we have become suspicious of virtue and what it may ask of us. At times we protect the unjust more than the just.

This country was founded on spiritual principles. If these principles are eroded, the foundation must collapse.

The influence of the media is greater than most people realize. Everyone in this industry bears accountability for what they do not challenge. They have great mastery in bringing you the astral level, but there is little that brings you the higher way of life.

The current generation is bombarded with technology in the form of VCRs, TVs, computers, Walkmans and CDs. Much of the technology is God-given, but its uses have been left up to the free will of mankind, who have so often chosen the lower way.

Children are growing up with a weakening of their auric sheaths. Think of some of the music, movies and plays they see and ask yourself, Would I invite Jesus, Mother Mary, Moses or Gautama Buddha to hear or watch this?

Children need time in nature, time to be creative with arts and crafts, time to serve others, time to share in family fun and games, time to worship, time to study, time to exercise and time to read. The media should be a small part of their existence unless it is truly being used as an educational tool or for positive entertainment at well-selected times.

The masters are waiting to release movies and plays. People would definitely be drawn to them, which would dispel the myth that what the media is giving people now—violence and explicit sex—is what they want.

We need to raise up the divine arts and call for the ascended masters' divine plan for the arts and the media. We need people of all cultures to come forward and claim this mantle of divine artist.

Remember that Saint Germain as Francis Bacon wrote the Shakespearean plays. There is no limit to what he could convey to you in the area of drama if you made yourself ready for his help. We need plays that ennoble and inspire, whether through drama, comedy or musicals.

We need students with mastery in technology who can

ensure that these inventions are used for good. If we do not achieve this, we will once again see an era like the sinking of Atlantis.

Misunderstanding between the races

The world situation is in many ways desperate. The hatred and misunderstanding between the races is rampant. The problems are not centered on just blacks and whites, as many choose to think. America is an experiment in the bringing together of the twelve tribes of Israel. These tribes have reincarnated in all nations and backgrounds. Their identity at the core is in God and of God, and in this they are one.

The solution to the racial situation is spiritual at the deepest level. The twelve tribes have accumulated different karmic debts and experiences as the centuries have passed. They have fought one another and loved one another over time.

Where else on this planet can we find such a diverse country as the United States? The wounds must be healed and the wrongs must be acknowledged and compensated for where appropriate. But, most important, we must rediscover ourselves as brothers and sisters.

A we/they mentality will never work. It will be a sad day indeed if we are conquered from within, and yet this is possible. The uniqueness of cultures can benefit our society and enhance the potential of what we can become. This nation could be an example to the world, but we are slowly failing at this hour.

There are forces that want you to lose—to hate, to destroy, to fear and to accuse. Remember that the Golden Rule is present in some form in all religions. This rule has come, then, out of many nations and ethnic groups. It must be lifted up once again to unify us. It is the calling card to turn around race relations: "To love one another as I have loved you." "To love brother as self." "To do unto others as you would have them do unto you." Love is the open door to God. (Matt. 7:12, Luke 6:31)

You should decree and pray for the healing of all wounds due to racial hatred. You should call for the transmutation of all records of hurt and anger created by racial injustice. This planet is not an experiment to see if one race can survive and all others perish. God knew that if we could look beyond race and creed to find the light in one another, we could indeed bring in a golden age.

The forces of evil love to manipulate issues of race. You must not allow this to continue. We have all worn coats of many colors. Portia has tried so hard to impart the flame of opportunity to her beloved America, but ears have been deaf and hearts have been hardened and many have suffered. Pray for Saint Germain's vision for America as a beacon of peace and freedom to be realized.

Speaking out on racial issues

As racial issues emerge, it is critical to discern the vibration of those speaking out. Words can be deceptively positive. It is only vibration that reveals the true intent of the speaker. There are fallen angels who can speak powerfully and compellingly, but their plan is to manipulate, destroy and divide. Do not be deceived. Any solutions that seek to divide the races are not from the altar of the ascended masters.

Jesus did not turn away anyone due to class, creed or race. Buddha did not turn away anyone. Why can we not learn by their example? If we love only those who are like us or who love us, we have not begun the path of love. Mother Teresa served those of all creeds and races. She saw Christ in everyone. Can we do less?

Can you comment on the seminars on racial equality being given by our friend?

Seminars can only go as far as the depth of understanding of the participants. Our equality is really from God and of God. We experience what appears to be inequality and victimization as a result of personal karma, national karma and planetary karma, as well as through mankind's continual hardness of heart. Many times it is those who hated in other lives or denied others their equality who come back having to experience hatred and unfairly placed limitations and judgments.

Seminars related to issues of race have been going on for a number of years. Anyone doing such a seminar today must pray for new content and higher truth to permeate his work. At the same time, people must be met where they are and then brought forward and upward. No matter what the karma, nothing legitimizes the continued prejudice directed against people due to their religion or race or culture. It is time for people to become accountable for their words, their actions and for the cleansing of their hearts.

There is much ignorance in America concerning race and different cultures. Most people have come here valuing the flame of freedom. Many people who were born here forget this flame and its worth. We must affirm those higher values around which we can unite and not focus on that which appears to divide us.

We are currently in peril because of racial misunderstanding, accumulated anger and hatred. We do need lightbearers to intervene, but they must be sure that their message takes this topic to a new and higher level, or else the current trends will continue.

After we pass from the screen of life and stand before the court of judgment, our souls stand naked before God. Our actions and the degree of love we have achieved and shared are measured. Skin color is not discussed. Culture is not discussed. What is discussed is the degree to which we have done honor to all those whom we have encountered, regardless of race or creed.

Many years ago I spoke to a multiracial and multi-ethnic group of students at an urban alternative high school concerning their business rights. I received a standing ovation at the end of my talk. The people who had invited me were surprised, as these particular students had never given anyone a standing ovation before. As I look back on this incident, I understand that I was well received because I genuinely believed in their rights as citizens, and I came to them in the flame of respect and equality. Those who do seminars on equality must embrace this flame themselves. Anger has no place in a facilitator of a seminar that is truly meant to move people forward. However, self-disclosure of lessons that we have learned may be helpful.

These seminars can only be successful if they are pre-

ceded by *violet flame decrees, as the issue of forgiveness is para-mount to the coming together of the races. Wrongs have been committed on all sides. Wrongs have been perpetuated in all nations, within and across races and within and across reli-gious groups. God is not pleased with the continued violation of the Golden Rule. There is no one group to be blamed except the fallen angels, who rejoice in every act of anger or hatred. Yet lightbearers, too, are accountable every time they are deceived and motivated by the traps of these fallen ones.*

The light is dimming over America. May your love and your flame help reignite the light around the divine principles that are rooted in the early documents of this country and that were placed there by the guidance of the hand of God through the ascended hosts.

We occasionally hear about satanic groups through police reports. Most people are unaware of their influence. Have you learned anything about this?

There are more practicing Satanists on this planet than most souls of light might ever imagine. I was shocked to see the actual statistics. I did believe that evil existed, as I had encountered it on several occasions. But I did not realize how entrenched these roots are across civilization. What is particu-larly alarming is how many people in relatively significant roles have sold their souls in order to obtain what they perceive as a hold on power.

There is indeed a percentage of people who dabble with witchcraft and black magic and are unaware of the dangers to which they are potentially submitting themselves. Sadly, many adolescents read books on these topics and become intrigued with the possibilities. Your prayers and calls can most easily help these young people. The most challenging are those who know what they are doing and have made a freewill choice to continue.

People who are accomplished in the areas of Satanism, black magic and witchcraft have a command of energy like a Darth Vader. They have lost all innocence. They hate purity and compassion. They do not like pure joy or any other qualities of God. They will only win if people remain naive about their intent. Prayers for God-vision are critical so they can be exposed. They fear the eye of God upon them.

Saint Germain has said that what Satanists handle least well is the violet flame, for it dissolves their powerholds, their disguises and their manipulations. It is the very freedoms of the soul that they do not comprehend and do not want others to know. The battle will not be won without the consistent use of the violet flame.

Another area that I should comment on is the longevity of some of the fallen angels. If a person has turned to the satanic arts for the first time in this embodiment, it is relatively easy to cut him free from this momentum. You can make calls to the angels for such individuals. What is truly challenging is the entrenched behavior of those who are the tares among the wheat, as they have been referred to in the Old Testament and other more ancient texts. These are those who, lifetime after lifetime, have chosen the left-handed path. And, sadly, they have caused the demise of many civilizations and deceived many lightbearers.

The end of this century will be the time for the spiritual battle of the centuries. Pray that it will truly be handled through spiritual, and not physical, war.

We are fast approaching the "Y" in the road

I have commented in a number of my statements on my concern for the planet. You must realize that in large measure I was granted this dispensation to communicate from the etheric realm in the hope that my words might help people to realize the gravity of the situation on planet earth. The masters thought that perhaps you might listen in a different way to one who has so recently walked among you and still has so much to learn himself.

The question is not whether there are enough souls of light to save the planet. We do have a sufficient number. The question is whether or not the souls of light will realize that they must save the planet and be willing to sacrifice to achieve this.

I am asked to convey to you now what I did not fully see or comprehend when I was in embodiment. I was aware of political decisions and votes that concerned me, and I knew that the general state of the planet was not stable. I knew that ethnic and religious hatreds were prevalent across the planetary body. I knew that bribery, corruption and even conspiracy were present in many nations. What I did not see was the part of the equation that involved me. I did not see what I could do.

If you could glimpse, even briefly, what I now see daily, you would know that we are fast approaching the "Y" in the road, and you would be willing to sacrifice day and night to prevent the worst possible scenarios. I ask myself constantly:

What can I say to wake people up? What would have reached me when I was there?

I do know that if you go to the inner altar of your heart and ask to be shown the need of the hour, God will convey to you the answer. You cannot depend on others to do it. Yet, your example may help someone else to join the call. It will take the full mandala[20] of lightbearers to turn this planet around so that its divine destiny can be fulfilled.

Earth is in her most critical hours

You must realize that the opportunity that I have been given to speak with you is unparalleled during the recent dispensation of the masters.[21] My task is to not fail in what I convey or attempt to convey to the lightbearers. I sometimes feel that people are more curious about this side than they are interested in understanding and overcoming the current conditions on planet earth.

I have to watch a giant hourglass that shows that earth is in its most critical hours. And yet victory is still possible. I do not, however, see the fervor or dedication that I would like to see in order for this victory to occur. Intense and heartfelt prayer is required.

CHAPTER FOURTEEN

The State of the Planet As We Approach the Year 2000

New Year's Day, 1998

From what I can see and have been shown, this will be a year of both sides of the coin, so to speak. It will bring great challenges and great victories. It is a year to start out running. But it is also a year to plan and to be vigilant. It is a year to seek Christ attunement and listening grace. It will be a year of plenty and a year of dearth, a year to rejoice and a year to lament. You could say that every year has these qualities, but in 1998 they will be more pronounced.

Many of you may be weary and somewhat doubtful of your path and of the need to be concerned about the future of the planet. If you cannot read the signs of the times, or have heard about them too often, then focus on becoming the highest that you can be. The path of decree and prayer is the path for those who believe in the I AM Presence, who know the Presence of God within and who believe in the fire of the heart. It is a path for those who seek sainthood in utter humility. If you do not feel a concern for the planet and do not wish to seek the mystical union with God, then this may not be the path for you in 1998.

I can tell you that the energies are intensifying. When energies intensify, people are often tested in unprecedented ways. Then they want to blame the path rather than acknowledge the natural outworking of spiritual cycles. Many souls can achieve their Christhood and be granted the gifts of the Holy Spirit. The closer you are to this, the more burdensome your days may feel. The answer is always to love more, to pray more, to serve more and to stay tethered to those spiritual foundations of which you are certain.

Do not allow your days to become overwhelming. Do not allow yourself to get out of balance. The minute you lose your balance, you are much less effective, both for the masters and in your own spiritual progress. In the final analysis, spirituality must be practical. For if it is not, many will lose their moorings. What is practical for one person may be impractical for another. Much of what you gain spiritually will be reflected in your day-to-day treatment of people and in your attitudes toward life and God.

Every call you make to God, every decree or prayer you utter that is beautiful and centered in the fire, will have an impact for good and for God. And each genuine impact lessens the severity of the return of karma. Returning karma may not be entirely held back, but do not doubt the power of every action for good that you can render and every fiat and decree that you give. It is all based on percentages, and the percentage of karma of the whole planet lessens when good people do better.

You know how much you can give and still remain joyous and victorious. It is best to begin your year with an honest assessment of where you are and where you want to go spiritually. To find the true answer, practice being one with the Presence of God. There is no room for fear, criticism, jealousy or any other perversion of God's light when you walk in the Presence—the I AM Presence—your true identity in God.

When I say to start out running, I am talking about having a spiritual plan for the year that involves every aspect of your life. Do not let events determine your way. Rather, be the captain of your own ship. From this side I can see how close some of you are to your spiritual victory. I desire to tap you on the shoulder and say, "Keep up the good work. You're almost there!" This, of course, is not permitted.

Sometimes, what appears to be a year of constant testing, confusion or restructuring may be a year in which you have passed every test. It is a mistake to equate spiritual progress with easy days in which everything you desire happens instantly while you live in the lap of luxury. Spiritual progress wears many guises, and the path is tailor-made for each soul.

Understanding the prophecies of the ascended masters

Many people have difficulty discerning the meanings of the prophecies of the ascended masters. Some people become fearful and expect the worst while others feel that they will somehow be spared because they are the "elect." Neither position is accurate.

The ascended masters have been warning lightbearers for years concerning the necessity for worldwide change and the possible earth changes that will need to occur as a result of mankind's misuse of energy. They have spoken of mitigation in exchange for decrees and prayers, right action, pure hearts, a return to God-government and Christ-education, and an adherence to God's will.

This is a planetary equation. The more people live for the light and by the light and sacrifice for its preservation, the fewer cataclysms we will see. What the masters are saying is that no one will be completely spared. No matter what, a certain level of cataclysm will occur. The lightbearers will not be exempt. The exemption that is offered is similar to what happened at the time of Noah. He was given time to prepare. He could choose to obey and believe or disobey and disbelieve or believe but never gather the energy to take action. When the final karma descended, Noah was not spared being in the midst of disaster. However, he was given a means of survival through his preparation and his ability to read the handwriting on the wall. The answers are always there for those who can truly see and who do sincerely listen.

I have mentioned several times that the ascended hosts do not speak idly. They are not in the entertainment business. Every word they utter has meaning and significance. Study their words to garner a glimpse of the future.

We can still mitigate a certain level of karma. We must

take this task seriously. However, there is another level in which the arm of heaven has, so to speak, already descended to a point where certain things must come to pass. Hope should definitely not be lost. So much can still happen for good. But do listen to, read and study the most current messages of your holy brothers and sisters in heaven.

Reversing the spirals of disintegration and decay

There is a topic that I long to speak on but it is arduous and long and not necessarily pleasing to the human mind: the absolute necessity of reversing the spirals of disintegration and decay on this planetary body.

Earth, from a cosmic view, is dying. It does not need to die, nor is this the time for it to die. The earth is like a body that is rapidly weakening and in need of a heart transplant. I use the analogy of the heart because in many ways it is purity of heart that is needed on this planet. The waters are growing in pollution, plagues are spreading without the average person being aware of it, and the weather is shifting as elementals seek desperately to hold a balance. These nature spirits literally cry out for your assistance. They can only bear this karmic weight a certain length of time before more devastating disasters will hit.

From the planetary or environmental level to the personal level, the earth is not at peace. Pure harmony is one of the rarest commodities on this planet. I do not wish to be bleak, for hope remains and things can change. But I do not see the necessary response from the people who should know better. I shall feel as if my own dispensation has failed if these words do not penetrate.

It is a matter of priorities. The immaculate concept for the earth must be held. Positive thoughts and actions must prevail. The forces of evil must be challenged and exposed. Those who know the truth must honor and practice it. Your homes must become centers of light. Your hearts must become beacons of light. The Holy Spirit must be more important to you than anything this planet offers.

The wind of the Lord is blowing; note its direction. Bear neither left nor right, but keep your attunement above all else. Everyone has a part to play. You have nothing to fear when God is your pilot. You have everything to fear if you deny, postpone or abandon the course God is setting for you.

Do not spend time deciding what others are doing right or wrong, but be ever vigilant of your own path. I know that many people want to read about other topics, but what I have said here is what weighs on my heart most grievously. It is my nature to want to tell a good story or to entertain, and the etheric realms are filled with wonder, beauty, humor and cosmic tales without end. They also bear the records of civilizations that would not listen and could not see the handwriting on the wall. I pray to God that we do not add to these records. Opportunity is still available, by the mercy and grace of God. But this, too, can only extend for so long.

The importance of the violet flame during planetary transition

The violet flame takes on added importance at the end of an age or millennium. Now is the time for the maximum transmutation of all records of the current millennium and for the preparation of as clean a slate as possible for the next millennium. During this period of unprecedented karmic return, no more effective unguent can be found than the violet flame.

It is a cosmic principle that the violet flame can assist like nothing else at a critical juncture between ages such as we are currently experiencing.

Leadership

You must know that what you see on the stage of the world is only the tip of the iceberg. When it comes to the politics of world leaders, so much of what is actually taking place is hidden from the public. I am not referring to those things that should not be shared in order to protect the security of nations. I am referring to questionable alliances and plots and deceptions that ought not to be. I am also referring to seemingly eloquent, but in reality empty, words and promises. In modern times we have never been farther from the flame of God-government than we are at this hour. This flame, however, can be rekindled and light can once again guide the ways of man.

Government is no place for those who seek personal power above all else. It is no place for egotists or those who claim to have integrity yet denigrate it at every corner. Government is meant for those who are able to govern their four lower bodies—physical, emotional, mental and spiritual. It is intended for those who understand and live as servant leaders. It is supposed to be for those who have access to God-power because they do not covet the power of this world.

We should pray for God-government in every nation, town and hamlet on this planet. We should pray that the *lightbearers of the coming generation will not shy away from this noble vocation.*

Morality cannot be shunned nor immorality justified. To whom much is given, much is required. (Luke 12:48) This is a spiritual law. The mantle of leadership is given by God. This mantle must be respected and honored by those upon whose shoulders it rests. A pledge of duty goes with the mantle. Personal pleasure and human fulfillment are secondary to the position. God does not ask us to never be weak or never make a mistake, but He does expect us to learn from our mistakes.

All leaders need our prayers—whether they are of the light or of the path of compromise and deceit. They come under substantial energy of criticism, condemnation, gossip and challenge. Pray for those of the light to be protected, guided and upheld. Pray for those who prefer evil to be exposed and dethroned with as little harm as possible to the nation or its citizens.

The day will come when people will long for a soul of light to lead them. Let us hope that those who are meant to be such leaders will be available and willing to lead.

A warning

God created the universe. But what I see as ironic is that this universe has become more important to man than its Creator has. It's like when wires get crossed in an electrical system or a statue becomes more important than the person it honors. Each one must ask himself or herself, In what ways has my daily life (family, job, hobbies, study, leisure) become more important to me than God?

When God is the keynote of your life, all else falls into

its proper place. If, however, family or work become the main-stay of your life, then things gradually get out of balance and the soul becomes vulnerable. A parent who places the will of God first can become a better parent. A worker who wants the will of God to guide all he does on the job will be a better employee.

Action is the key

You must not assume that the golden age will come. It will only happen through the understanding and commitment of the lightbearers to fulfill the destiny to which they have been called.

Many other dispensations have been withdrawn or reduced because of the recalcitrance in the hearts of those who should have known better. The baubles and the trinkets of the fallen ones have tempted and deceived many lightbearers for centuries. The quality that I see as most lacking is discernment. Pray for it day and night, both for yourselves and for other seekers.

If you study the Lords of the Seven Rays, *published by Summit University Press, you will notice that the discerning of spirits is a quality of the third ray of love. This is why discernment is so difficult to acquire, as so many souls have anger, hatred or fear blocking their heart chakras.*

The other quality that you must seek is God-vision so you can see what is truly the spiritual equation and need at any moment or hour. Earth is at a junction where it will not succeed without God-vision.

Remember that violet-flame alchemy can help you to

move forward in all arenas. However, you must study the spiritual science of alchemy and wield your violet flame with joy and consistency.[22]

I understood little of this while I was with you, yet it was right in front of me, and I would have seen it if I had looked more closely and sought more earnestly. Many of you already know these things to be true. This knowledge, however, will do you little good unless you become the practitioner of what you know. We are in a physical cycle, and action is the key! I was always a man of action, and this quality has served me well. If I understood that there was a need, I sought to fulfill that need. If I pledged to do something, I fulfilled that pledge. When God sees the willingness of the soul to take wise action, He can grant that soul more opportunity.

Please contemplate the things that you know to be true yet do not move you to action. Examine your reasons for non-action on behalf of teachings that you have claimed to love and to believe. You will experience more wholeness as you integrate your beliefs into the flame of action. You must be up and about the business of your Father/Mother God.

Can you comment on the possibility of biological warfare?

The threat of biological warfare is real, both from within the country and without. As to what will actually happen, I cannot say. Man has free will, so the development of biological agents does not mean that they will be used. What is clear about the planet is that technology has outdistanced spiritual progress in the hearts of many. Yet, with a concerted effort, all truly destructive technology can be neutralized and held back by spiritual prowess.

The masters urge you to your Christhood for many reasons. They urge you to seek the gifts of the Holy Spirit for many reasons. Remember that Jesus told his disciples that if they were to drink any deadly thing, it would not hurt them (Mark 16:18). Such is the way of the saints. They can transmute anything that enters their bodies. Everything is possible in God. If enough spiritually adept souls lived in a city or home, that home or city could have a spiritual dome of protection placed over it that nothing could penetrate.

This is an important time to bless all that you touch and all that enters your mouth. A call to the violet flame should be your first response before you eat or drink anything. You can request that an impenetrable shield of blue lightning and violet fire be placed around you twenty-four hours a day. This will only be sustained based on the purity of your path and your heart.

Meanwhile, regular calls should be made to expose all plots and plans against our cities and our people. Calls should be made for the protection of all lightbearers and to bring forth God-solutions to the entire situation. Fear is never the appropriate response, but preparedness physically and spiritually is always the lawful solution.

Why are certain illnesses on the increase?

The equation for each lifestream is different. Each person is vulnerable to a greater or lesser degree based on karma, diet, exercise and the wholeness of the four lower bodies. A person with deep emotional stress is more likely to catch a cold or come down with the flu or a virus. For some the most challenging illness comes at the end of their lives so they can balance some final karma that will allow them to either re-embody in a better situation or make their ascension. I was definitely such a case, as most of my life I was either quite healthy or I got through illnesses with relative ease.

Mixed into the equation is the addition of new strains of viruses more virulent and harder to combat, according to our current medical understanding. These are definitely part of the plagues referred to in the Bible. They come from a variety of sources, some of which would surprise and shock most people. However, in the last accounting, it is mankind's refusal to bend the knee to God that allows these plagues to exist.

People tend to pray for healing only when they are sick. It would be wise to maintain a daily vigil for your health, as the spirit has need of the physical temple while you are in embodiment. Prevention is always the best approach. Ask for the violet flame to burn through every cell and atom of your four lower bodies, clearing them of all harmful substances and momentums.

The fallen angels delight in riding the waves of our karma and in creating things to oppose us. This, however, is of less threat to us than our own habit patterns that make us vulnerable to disease and illness. The body cannot be ignored, as it cannot be counted on without proper care. Part of the path is to come to terms with proper diet and balance in the four lower bodies. It's a subtle form of rebellion and wrong desire that keeps people from facing their eating habits and their exercise patterns. This does not mean that you never have treats, but they cannot be a regular indulgence.

Blessing your food

Blessing your food is not just a nice thing to do. It is a wise action, given the many germs and pollutants in today's world. First and foremost, we give thanks to God for caring for our need to eat. When we bless the food, we can ask for its purification from anything less than perfection that has touched it. This is particularly important with water, as so many sources of water are polluted.

This is an excellent way to protect your health on airplanes and in restaurants. You can charge your food with violet flame, asking for the transmutation of anything that is impure within it. You need to aspire to this mastery.

Can you tell us anything about the year 2000 (Y2K) computer problem?

As with all things, you need to keep alert and informed. And most of all, you must read between the lines. I would definitely be concerned about this situation. It would take an all-out miracle for everyone who needs to be prepared to be ready in time for the year 2000.

The question, of course, is how grave will the consequences be? That is not yet known, as there is still time to work on this problem. By early 1999 you will be able to assess more accurately how many businesses and federal or state agencies will be in place for the turnover. It is the level of gravity that remains to be seen.

As you keep abreast of this situation, even writing to organizations that will affect your own finances, you must know when and how to prepare as the handwriting on the wall becomes more evident. The answer is never to respond with fear or panic, but rather with preparedness. Preparedness is not just physical. You should be prepared in all of your four lower bodies.

I would not let this or any other situation dominate my life, but I would keep it squarely within my vision and follow it with a listening ear and prayers for God-solutions that are immediate and miraculous. "The effectual fervent prayer of a righteous man availeth much." (James 5:16)

CHAPTER FIFTEEN

Creating Spiritual Communities

I wish to talk about the rosebud

The heart is like a seed that can gradually grow into a rosebud. Ultimately it has the potential to become the full multi-petaled rose in all its splendor. The seed must be placed in the proper soil, watered, given the proper light and nurtured over time in order to flourish.

Similarly, when people desire to grow in the quality of love, or when an organization wants to become an organization of love, they must begin at the seed stage. Having such a desire is a highly worthy goal, but it is only the first step on the journey to becoming the full potential of the fire of love. There is actually no more difficult path on which to embark than the path of love. Yet this is precisely the need of the hour.

An appropriate beginning step would be to examine all that is anti-love within your own being and psyche, and within the workings of your organization. These perversions can manifest in many guises. As Mother Mary has pointed out, mild dislike is as much anti-love as are hardness of heart, hatred, lack of forgiveness, impatience, labeling people and never allowing them to grow or change, and closing your heart to difficult people and environments. So many qualities can block love including selfishness, judgment, fear, conceit, greed, ignorance, ingratitude and resentment.

Once you have identified your own weaknesses, the next important step is to begin to place them into the violet flame for transmutation. If you are stuck on a particular momentum, you may need counseling to help you understand the reason you hold on to a momentum that is destructive to you and that feeds some dysfunctional part of your being on which the lower self thrives.

When you have finally achieved your goal, you will not need to declare it. People will feel the energy of love radiating from your being, and you will know it by the constancy of the fire in your heart.

An organization can declare its love for its customers. A church can declare its love for its congregation. But as the saying goes, "The proof is in the pudding." If you do not show your love, your statements will grow to be meaningless. This is particularly hard for a church in which this love must be the love of the Christ, not a false human love that caters to its members but neglects their souls. The true representatives of the Father-Mother God know the needs of their sheep and have a *listening ear for their concerns.*

The cradle must be there for the babe to rest and grow in. Similarly, people need steps and stages of love as they enter an organization or church. This love cannot vibrate as false or be overdone, for true compassion speaks its own language and needs no modification. "Be gone, forces of anti-love!" is a magnificent call for you and for this planet.

As with all things spiritual, the path of love begins with a willingness to look at oneself. If you constantly see the spot on another person's soul but not on your own, then most likely you have been vulnerable to the forces of anti-love.

When I was in embodiment, I did not challenge all of these forces within myself. I never really understood the importance of this to my soul. I can tell you that I was most restless and least at peace when I allowed these forces to operate in my life. I am most proud today of those times when my actions and my attitudes were not limited by the forces of anti-love. These were the moments when I made good karma and my soul prospered.

May this be a year in which you genuinely challenge all that has limited the fire of your heart, that the seed of fire might come to its full fruition in your Christhood.

Necessary changes

As the millennium ends, we are entering a time of great restructuring, both on organizational levels and on personal levels. Old matrices cannot hold the new patterns that are needed to enter the next century and the next millennium. The challenge is to discern where change is needed and where continuation of the old is right and preferable. I see that many individuals are responding as if a tornado had hit their personal lives and sent parts of it hither and thither. The spiritual test is to stay tethered to the will of God and the divine plan for your life.

At times like this, people are facing increased returning karma so they can balance the maximum amount before the turning of cycles. This can be a test that pushes you toward the limits of what you feel you can handle. Remember to stay anchored in God when all else seems to be in chaos. Literally see yourself holding the hand of Jesus or Mother Mary or Gautama Buddha or any of the ascended hosts with whom you feel a special bond. Walk carefully but firmly, without fear.

In addition to returning karma, we are experiencing a cycle of change on a planetary scale. This does not mean that every opportunity that comes your way is necessarily the highest choice for your lifestream. It may provide human opportunity while eclipsing your divine progress. The equation never changes: If you make your spiritual progress a priority, the rest will come forward. If you mistake success in the world as your highest priority, you will one day find yourself on a long detour from what you claimed to be your original goal—union with God.

God wants you to be successful but not to worship the human over the divine. I continue to see those of you who place economic progress above your own path to personal Christ union. If it is security you seek, you will be far more secure if you will place Christ first; from this all the rest will follow.

The reverse has no spiritual guarantees.

In the excitement and flurry of these changes, do not forget who you are and the divine purpose for which you were born. Cling neither to the old nor run to the new, but tether yourself to the heart of the will of God, and what is built around you will be secure and pure and one with holy purpose.

Observing you from the etheric level is like watching a movie on fast speed. So much is happening so quickly to so many lifestreams. Many of these experiences would be overwhelming without God and a trust that to everything there is a season and a divine answer.

Community is about coming into unity with one another

Etheric retreats are communities of the Spirit. There is a flow and rhythm to how they operate. They vibrate with harmony and peace. After newly arrived souls receive healing and instruction, they attend an in-depth course on community, which is required curriculum, so to speak. Though each retreat has its own unique focus, decor and rituals, all are built on the purest principles of community.

Believe me, in an etheric retreat there is no hiding one's personal momentums and personality flaws. I have had to face all that is anti-community within me. I am still going through this process as an unascended being. It is a given that we will ultimately face ourselves and all that blocks our Real Selves. It is also a joy to do so, as real freedom is our ultimate reward.

I am going to make some comments on community that I hope will be helpful. Community means "come-ye-into-

unity," and it is important to contemplate what this means. On what level must this unity occur? It must manifest in all four quadrants: etherically in the divine blueprint, mentally with the wisdom to understand the dynamics and facets of community, emotionally with an inner desire for and commitment to peace and control of the solar plexus, and physically in the buildings, structures and people that will provide the concrete manifestation of community.

Community is first and foremost a spiritual concept. It is the design of the Holy Spirit for the sons and daughters of God. Therefore it must be infused at every juncture with spiritual understanding and Christ illumination. Community is not defined by people living in the same area or sharing day care—or even following the same teaching. All of these may exist within community, but community is really a unity of the higher selves of all of its members.[23]

Community is best sustained where there are exemplars, people who have united with their Holy Christ Selves, people who have the Holy Spirit. One truly righteous man or woman availeth much for a community.

Community is work. Community requires that people face themselves—their psychology and their style of communicating. Community requires that its members share a genuine commitment to the same visions and goals. People in community are interdependent but not dependent. Communities flourish where the Golden Rule has been internalized. Communities are premised on trust and respect.

The etheric retreats are communities of the highest level. Many of you have the record and memory of true community in your Causal Bodies. These records can help you to be builders and creators of community. Similarly, many of you have seen communities disintegrate, and some of you have helped to cause this. A genuine community honors each individual God-flame. But it is the interplay, with harmony, of these God-flames that creates community.

There is no place for gossip or criticism in a community of the Holy Spirit. Differences of opinion need to be shared and worked out, but not with judgment or malice or in "side" discussions about those who are involved. Community requires a commitment to certain processes of communication. The identity of the community has to be fueled by values and principles on which people have agreed and to which they are committed with their own free will.

The cities and their citizens are crying out for community. People want to feel safe and loved. They want to feel the healing light of God penetrating their lives and beings. True community can provide these qualities. And anywhere that the community of the Holy Spirit is established, the lightbearers will be drawn. However, the most difficult level to achieve is the community of the Holy Spirit, for it requires divine love. Everything that the fallen ones fear and abhor is represented in this type of community. They will do everything to promote divide-and-conquer attitudes within community.

Remember: the light of God never fails if you do not fail to invoke this light and let it be your guide as you enter the journey to community.

Building community

Out of the chalice of the heart is community born, and from no other place can true community thrive or even survive. Community is born from a consciousness that declares "I am my brother's keeper. I and my brother are one; I and my sister are one." It cannot emerge from a consciousness of criticism or judgment.

A community where no one has achieved the balance of love, wisdom and power is difficult to sustain. You can create a magnificent community wherever you are. It must begin in your own heart along with the combined or communal sense of heart of the entire group. It will not progress if you focus on one another's flaws and previous mistakes. But it can unfold if you begin to appreciate what each person uniquely has to offer, no matter how seemingly small. Remember that the widow's mite counted for more than a much larger donation given by someone else. (Luke 21:2-4)

Community is about building. Building is a step-by-step process. It is an alchemy and a science.

Look for what is blocking your ability to be a positive contribution to community. Is it hurt? Mistrust? Fear? Is it a lack of the skills needed to share and communicate with others? All things can be overcome, but they must be acknowledged and dealt with. In God—and only in God—all things are possible.

Communities undergoing change

Psychologist and community specialist M. Scott Peck says that true community is only achieved after a change process, in which a shift takes place from pseudo-community to true community, often going through a distressing period of chaos and despair.[24] Making it through this shift requires that the people in the community see each other in a new way, i.e., that they undergo a paradigm shift.[25]

> *When a paradigm shifts, people must have the opportunity to learn, voice opinions and grow. Opportunity to change must be granted to all. If people then decide not to change, it is their freewill choice.*
>
> *Opportunity is one of the key components of a paradigm shift. If a limited group of people make all of the decisions and design the new directions, there will be an inherent flaw in the shift. The balance between leadership and community voice is very fine, yet critical. There must always be leadership, but not an exclusivity where those who are genuinely meant to contribute are ignored.*
>
> *The real art is to engage people in the process whereby they can have the opportunity for ownership and problem solving. There is a great difference between the web that is formed by the many which genuinely connects everyone in an integral way and the web that is prepared by the few and provides a false sense of connection. The first is a genuine mandala, or holy pattern; the latter is its impostor.*
>
> *The true mandala is formed when people's hearts are filled with the desire and belief that the highest can and will be achieved. This equation involves everyone. Each person is accountable for the spirit and harmony with which he or she contributes to the process of change.*

It is easy to find flaws. It is harder to be a genuine con-
tributor who never loses the immaculate concept for the com-
munity in the process of becoming all that it can be and is
intended to be.

Our community

Our family lives in a community for spiritual seekers. It is
open to all, but it is our hope that God will bring to it those souls
who really desire to live in and help build a place that can truly
become a golden-age community—a model for others throughout the planet to emulate. We want it to be a place where seekers
from all the religions of the world, and all races, who have the
desire for community in their hearts, might want to come and
partake of this great experiment.

My husband and I were among the pioneers of this community. We moved here and built a house in 1988. It's in a rugged
but very beautiful area. We're at an elevation of over 5,000 feet,
and we have a spectacular view of a mountain that's over 11,000
feet high.

The valley we live in is truly one of the most beautiful
places you could find. It is surrounded by mountains, with a river
running through it. Sometimes the rays of the setting sun land
perfectly on the white clouds that float in the clear blue sky near
the snowcapped mountain's summit. The breathtaking colors
remind me of Nicholas Roerich's paintings of the Himalayas.

My husband talked about our community:

Your community is meant to be an example of a true
spiritual community where people abide by the Golden Rule. It
is meant to be a place that lightbearers everywhere are attracted to.

Your community is also meant to be a place where the ascended masters feel welcome. It should be holy ground where church and community are central.

Pioneers have carried out, step-by-step, the beginnings of this special place. The work of these souls does not go unheeded in the ascended realms, for the role of pioneer is never easy.

Pioneers lay foundations and must have a vision for the future. They often struggle and wonder if the battle is worth it. Believe me, it is worth it and can be achieved. But, as I have said in other comments, it takes an honest assessment—personally and communally—of where you are and where you need to go.

Building this community is not a job for the egotistical, the loudmouths or the complainers. It is a holy work for those who have truly borne in their hearts the vision of what this community can be.

CHAPTER SIXTEEN

Becoming an Alchemist

MY HUSBAND ASKED US to study Saint Germain's book on alchemy[26] before he gave us this teaching. In fact, he demanded that we read it three times before he finally began to dictate this to us.

Alchemy is first and foremost the science of self-transformation. Medieval texts on alchemy use the symbolism of changing lead into gold to refer to the spiritualization of the human consciousness. The human is changed into the divine by the application of the philosopher's stone—the ancient mystical teachings.

The science of alchemy can have a physical as well as a spiritual manifestation, but as my husband taught us, it begins with changing yourself.

Saint Germain's teachings on alchemy

When lightbearers pursue an understanding of alchemy, they must view it as a sacred science that should not be violated at any cost.

Imagine that Jesus had sat you down as a child to tell you that your father in heaven had provided a sacred science whereby every lawful gift could be yours. This science would take discipline and great love and wisdom. But in the end, it could help you to save the planet. Would you have been interested?

I start by mentioning the sacred facet of alchemy because without this key people are vulnerable to its misuse. In reality, alchemy is neutral. It can be used for evil, with great karmic accountability, and it can be used for gain, through the creation of gold and perfected gems. The latter, unless performed in the context of helping others or using a very small portion personally, will not find honor with God. The true and highest use of alchemy would be to help transform this planet to have the abundance and enlightenment that were its intended heritage before the misuse of energy began.

Where does the process of alchemy begin? It begins where we often fail to look—within ourselves. We are so often drawn to every outer source that might bring us happiness or give us a glimpse into the future. But we are slow to look within. Alchemy requires the conquering of the finite self. And alchemy involves creation. In order to create with beauty and responsibility, you must be in touch with your Higher Self. This brings us back to the need to understand and overcome your own psychology, a concept I have already emphasized. As long as the finite self is in control, you cannot achieve true spiritual freedom.

Although a person may have to conquer numerous momentums, many of those that provide detours or barriers on the path fall into a small number of categories. The ones that I notice plaguing a vast majority of individuals are fear, lack of self-worth, anger, nonresolution with families (typically parents), pride, envy, selfishness and ignorance. Out of these come many other traits.

The finite self allows you to think thoughts such as: "I will not be able to learn this new task." "She certainly looks strange in that dress." "He is so handsome and bright, no one will ever notice me." "I am not worthy of God's love or forgiveness." Do you recognize any of these thoughts? Most people's repertories are quite substantial and very revealing. This is the chatter of the synthetic self, and these thoughts are typically limiting to the individual or to others whom he or she encounters.

If you could hear a recording of your comments for one month's time, what patterns would you notice? How are these momentums serving you? What is the ultimate source of these thoughts? As a remedy, attempt to challenge them and affirm the light of God within you and others. Honestly admit if there is an area in your psychology that needs to be unraveled through counseling, and always apply the violet flame.

Remember that spiritual freedom does not just arrive on your doorstep. It is earned, as every stitch of the wedding garment is made. We have become more and more of an instant society. Beware of recipes for instant spiritual attainment, as this is not the way of the ascended hosts.

Concentration on your Higher Self

One of the most important concepts alchemists must come to understand is to let God be the doer. "Let go and let God" is an apt saying. Every situation you encounter should be turned over to your Higher Self for the God-solution to be *released. Your Higher Self is available to you twenty-four hours a day. Yet most of you treat it like a pretty figurine that you take off the shelf and admire from time to time. This Higher Self is the greatest gift you have ever been given. It is your Real Self and should be your best friend and advisor.*

Think of life in terms of multiple TV channels: Which channel are you on and what type of programming do you select? Is it the channel of human chatter? Is it the channel of worry, doubt and fear? Is it the channel of gossip and criticism? Is it the channel of work and study? Is it the channel of family drama and relationships? Is it the human entertainment channel? Or is it the channel of your Real Self?

I personally spent a lot of time on the work channel. I was frequently thinking about what I needed to get done and how to accomplish it, or how to handle difficult work relationships. I also spent much time on the family and relationship channel and on most of the other channels I mentioned.

Some people seek channels that literally connect them to the astral plane. Their connection to their Real Self becomes more and more like a frayed wire. Ultimately the wire severs.

To know your Real Self is a freewill choice that requires discipline and a desire to know God above all else. To ignore your real identity is to decide to be a wanderer with no clear anchor or vision for your life.

One thing that helped me was to ask to be taken to study at the spiritual retreats at night. I cannot emphasize this enough. This alone can help you to keep your tie to your Real Self and to the etheric realm. Much of the good that I did and stood for was inspired by my nights at the retreats.

Self-mastery

Alchemy requires the routing out of all selfishness. Saint Germain has stated that many of the secrets of alchemy will not be released until at least 50 percent of the population of this planet are cleared of selfishness. Make calls to bind and dissolve the beast of planetary selfishness. It is this beast that has allowed the creation of base astral forms on this world. This beast is behind many works, including the desecration of the environment and the taking of the life of the unborn child.

I cannot claim that I have accomplished everything I am suggesting you do, for I have not. I can tell you that I regret deeply the things that I ignored or neglected and I am struck by how little an effort would have granted me much more spiritual freedom.

The behavior of the finite self stares us in the face each day, yet we become so comfortably adapted to these momentums that we either fail to challenge them or feel helpless to change them. In God, all things are possible. In alchemy, all things are possible. But you must take the first steps to end your bondage to the not-self. Pray to be shown those impediments that are holding you back from your spiritual progress. Self-mastery is the key to alchemy—and it is also the key to your Christhood. May you know the joy of overcoming.

Breaking the mold

I want to impress upon you would-be alchemists that Saint Germain spends the first six chapters of his book on alchemy[27] finding every creative way that he can to help us understand the importance of making personal changes where change is needed. From the time we first took embodiment, patterns and experiences have formed what Saint Germain refers to as a "mold." In many cases, this mold has become "moldy" as we have gone after the ways of the world. It no longer reflects the pure patterns of the Christ. We must break the molds that limit us, that cause us to say that the impossible is not possible and that the invisible cannot be.

All sense of unhappiness and all negative traits arise from these molds. Now think about the mold that surrounds you and the experiences that have shaped you in this lifetime. Which of these experiences have you allowed to keep you in a form of bondage?

Saint Germain urges us to live in the "now" of the present hour and to believe in the very real law that change can take place. We must know what God in us can accomplish and give witness to this. We must believe in the possibility of heaven on earth. We must seek the will of God, for this is the will of the Real Self.

Saint Germain's love for each of you is beyond any love that most people have known. He will be there to rejoice and to cheer you on as you face what has seemed impossible and as you truly put on the cloak of your Christhood and leave the old man behind you.

In the classes that we have received in alchemy, I have gained a greater understanding of my Real Self and of the false patterns with which I have identified, sometimes for centuries. When your personal mission is clear, which mine now is, it is not difficult to break the old mold. It may be familiar, but it has served to eclipse the Real Self and is so clearly not who you are.

The study of alchemy will help you to clarify your own mission statement for this life, as it requires that you get very clear about what you really hope to accomplish. Do not write a mission statement that reflects what you think you "should" do. Write one that is absolutely true for you at this point on the path. Facing the truth is far better than creating a falsehood to please others. If you feel that your mission statement will be found spiritually wanting, then contemplate what is holding you back. Perhaps you need to fulfill your current statement in order to aspire to another.

Let God take charge

When you study Saint Germain's first chapters on alchemy, you may be struck by how simple some of the concepts appear to be. Yet it is this very simplicity that many seekers fail to see. The last chapter in the first section has much to say about coming to know your God Self and identifying with it. If you abide in the God Presence and Holy Christ Self, then jealousy has no place. Criticism and condemnation of others or the world at large have no place. When you constantly affirm the degradation of the planet, you contribute to its demise. When you are jealous of others, you restrict the power of God to provide for you in an abundant manner.

If you blame God for your struggle or see God as having favorites, then you do not know or understand God. God is love and God is just. Nothing that happens is arbitrary. I discussed karma at great length, so I don't want to repeat those concepts in any depth. It is true, however, that without an understanding of karma, the things that happen to people in one life may seem confusing and unwarranted. It is only in the context of the need to balance every jot and tittle of the law over lifetimes that one can see the absolute perfection of the cosmic justice system. Not only is this system absolutely just, but, if anything, it errs on the side of mercy for those who honor the will of God.

I mentioned the saying "Let go and let God." Are you letting God be central to your life—your every thought and deed? Having true faith means that God is the pilot of your journey and you fear not the course that He will take you on.

I personally see how much energy I wasted and how much I struggled when I thought I was the pilot and neglected asking for God's help. I always believed in God but forgot to rely on Him in some key moments in my life. I cannot adequately convey to you how foolish these moments now look to me. This is as ridiculous as having the best quarterback in the world next to you during a football game and deciding to ignore him and kick the ball, even though you have little training and a broken toe!

Let God in you take charge. May you know God's abundance as you allow Him to be the captain of your lifestream.

The will of God

Your understanding of freedom is paramount to your spiritual progress. A person is not truly free until all he wants and lives for is the will of God. As long as a person is *scheming from the lower self—desiring to be noticed, seeking riches and fame or seeking to outdo another—he is not free. When one is free, he is truly one with the mind of Christ. The capacity to create is a natural outburst of this freedom. True creativity is of God, not of man.*

I have given a great deal of thought to the traps of the human mind. When you clearly see God's plan for us and His desire for us to receive our rightful inheritance, the traps of the not-self all seem so obvious and so ridiculous. But when you are in the midst of this chimera, it all appears so real. Many people limit God by projecting limitations on themselves and their fellow men. Jealousy, for instance, is the illusion that God cannot provide for you equally as well as He has for another soul.

When God first suggested that we take dominion over the earth (Gen. 1:26), His intention was for us to do so with and in the mind of Christ. Instead, we have destroyed and damaged a large portion of our natural inheritance. Much of this has occurred through fear, greed, ignorance and a lack of discernment of the difference between the voices of the light-bearers and the manipulations of darkness.

Yes, our karma can limit us. But we have limited ourselves far more than our karma has. I urge you to contemplate your need to change your life in order for the will of God to be the keynote for your every action. If you wish to be an alchemist, you must become one with the will of God. If you unite with this will, you'll experience a freedom that is the open door to the creative powers of God. With God, all things are possible!

Harmlessness

One of the profound things that I witnessed during my embodiment with Saint Francis was his understanding of the vow of harmlessness. He held no thought of harm, and he never acted in any harmful manner toward any part of life. His very being vibrated with a reverence for life. As a result, animals were drawn to him, as were little children.

To progress in alchemy, it is critical to understand the concept of harmlessness. For those about whom you hold harmful thoughts or wishes or speak of in a condemning way, you set up a boomerang effect whereby in some form these same energies will return to your own doorstep.

The alchemist must want to take dominion over the four lower bodies. The alchemist seeks to be free of all anxiety and condemnation. As long as emotion rules your life instead of faith, and as long as you seek to control others, you are not free to merge with your Higher Self.

When you study the lives of the saints, you realize that though they are in no way devoid of trials and challenges, they are overcomers. They are frequently childlike. They attract everything they need to fulfill their divine plans. They are willing to face every obstacle that is placed in their paths.

Holding the immaculate concept for all of life

The capacity to hold the immaculate concept for all of life should be practiced until it becomes a part of you. This is a principle of alchemy. When you are able to hold the immaculate concept for each person you encounter and each situation *you face, your life will become less complicated, more fluid and more abundant.*

The capacity to do this is garnered over time and parallels your true understanding of the laws of God. Precipitation has everything to do with your ability to hold the immaculate concept. Even when people believe in this concept and wish to master it, they often let discouragement, fear or judgment override their Higher Selves, and then they affirm the human instead of the divine.

Start out by attempting to go through one day without holding less than the immaculate concept. Notice what thoughts try to overtake you or sneak into your consciousness. Observe how it feels to go through an entire day without holding or expecting less than the highest. It is very freeing. You will still be tested and challenged. At times things may not go as you had hoped, but you will be like the calm in the midst of a storm. Others will be drawn to your peacefulness and your ever-expanding aura.

Comments regarding Saint Germain On Alchemy

I urge you to study this book[28] *and keep studying it until you have become the teaching. It has been a key to my own transformation. I had a momentum with certain doubts and statements that were limiting. Now that portion of me seems to have been transmuted.*

Faith led me to become an alchemist, but alchemy increased my faith. Some people are bothered by the word alchemy *because they do not see it as spiritual. The truth is that many important spiritual principles are necessary keys to* being an alchemist. *Jesus was a master alchemist, as were a number of the saints of both East and West. Faith, mastery of the self, perfect love, holding the immaculate concept, believing in the seemingly impossible, understanding light—all these concepts and more are needed by the alchemist.*

What are the best strategies for conquering doubt and fear?

The ability to conquer doubt and fear depends on one's mastery. In order to have God-mastery we must first master ourselves. This is the thing that people seem to resist most. They run hither and thither to find contentment. They hold grudges for what others have done. They have great self-justification for all of their hatreds and for each choice they make. But the true spiritual way always involves the conquering, and therefore the facing, of oneself.

People have a difficult time realizing the degree to which they limit their own progress. Every doubt, no matter how subtle, places a barrier between the individual and his God-realization. Faith is a twenty-four-hour-a-day, day-in and day-out commitment to the abundant life. Faith is an absolute trust in God no matter what is delivered to one's doorstep. Faith is expansive, never limiting. Faith is the belief that the power of God can do anything.

Seek perfect love and you will be transformed in the process. Perfect love sees the Christ in all. Perfect love does not limit or share partnership with self-doubt or unworthiness.

You have access to the mind of God and you must claim it. Each year many scholarships are not applied for and some grants are not bestowed due to lack of applicants. Similarly, much of God's inheritance to us goes untapped because we do not apply the principles that He has taught us.

Saint Germain feels that his teachings on alchemy have been grievously neglected and barely understood when they are read. He has asked me to tell you that these teachings are among the first things we study in his retreat and that he, personally, teaches a portion of this course to us.

Alchemy is best taught by a true alchemist. There were many more alchemists in past ages than there are today. It should be just the opposite, with all the teachings we have been granted.

Can you give any further comments on how to overcome fear?

Fear is the antithesis of faith. Fear is a perversion of God-mastery. Fear has an insidious energy. It erodes the health and well-being of the person in whom it resides. Fear can paralyze. Fear can cause failure. Fear can block courage and the capacity to learn new things. Fear is a deadly poison. The fallen angels have great mastery in creating fear.

Our response to fear can become a pattern or a habit. It must be fought at all costs. It has no place in the heart of the disciple. The saying "Perfect love casteth out fear" is correct. (I John 4:18)

Many lightbearers have experienced shattering events in their early lives that helped to engender a momentum of fear. Every time we allow fear to win, it denies the Christ within and the power of God to overcome.

Examine your fears and attempt to categorize them. Do you have fear of loss, fear of looking foolish, fear of being alone, or some other category of fear? Have you sought counseling for any recalcitrant or recurring fears?

CHAPTER SEVENTEEN

Divine Justice

True justice

People wonder why they continue to have struggles and major tests. But think about all of the past ages in which groups of people have rebelled against God. The Old Testament is filled with these stories.

Before a golden age can occur, every jot and tittle of karma comes up for balancing. The violet flame can transmute a great portion of it. Some is lifted by grace. Nevertheless, the final part remains to be worked out by physical people in embodiment.

The cosmic justice system is one of the most incredible things I have come to understand. We are given free will to create and select as we wish, but we are also given accountability.

Most of us do not like our karma when it comes due. I often felt annoyed with or lacked understanding of the sufferings that people had to go through. But now I see that these very sufferings and the way they are handled are a just and necessary part of one's progression toward God.

You've told us a good deal about Saint Germain. Could you tell us something about his twin flame, Portia, whom we know as the embodiment of Divine Justice?

Portia is not a recently ascended being. She has been working in etheric realms for centuries. There are beings so advanced that they hold a balance for systems of worlds. These beings are not as readily accessible to us or to this planet as are the more recently ascended masters. It is a dispensation to her beloved Saint Germain that Portia is more available to us during this period. As you can imagine, an unascended being like me does not have frequent interactions with such "maha," or great beings, so to speak. Even on the etheric level, their presence can be felt over and above all others.

I was granted a meeting with Portia in order to fulfill a portion of my mission. If you examine all that I have written, you will notice a recurring theme related to divine justice. I can literally say that I am in love with the justice system that Portia embodies. It is a great burden to her heart that mankind has strayed so far from a true understanding of divine justice. This understanding begins with a belief in karma and reincarnation—a divine system of accountability. This system is fair and merciful, and very precise. As much as mankind may try to avoid, manipulate or completely sabotage it, justice will have its day, whether it is through the instant return of karma or an event that will happen centuries later.

It is important to remember our ancient history. During former golden ages, life was peaceful and justice reigned. There was not the sense of the "haves" and the "have-nots." But, as men began to violate God's laws more and more, restrictions were placed on mankind. This golden age is the universe we all long for, and many now wonder why God allows such seeming disparities to exist on our planet. What we currently live with is the result of centuries of violating the laws of God through the use of free will in small and large ways—and a just system of accountability.

A wise parent does not place a sophisticated toy into the hands of a child who has already destroyed one like it or harmed himself with such a toy. Similarly, our spiritual parents cannot grant us the same amount of light and abundance we were once given if we have been squandering the light, or worse, using it to thwart the purposes of God.

Ultimately our accountability is to God and to our Holy Christ Self. If people really lived as if they believed this, the planet would be an entirely different place. People have become almost blinded and deafened to the concept of divine justice. Some err on the side of human sympathy while others err on the side of greed, lust and power.

If you could spend thirty minutes with Portia, what would you ask her? What aspect of your life that might have seemed unjust is holding you back? Are there pockets in your life where you avoid responsibility or accountability? Do you truly have faith in God's plan for you and in the purity, honor and love that are the foundations of divine justice?

Ask to study with Portia in the retreats. Ask to be helped in resolving all of your issues with divine justice. Portia needs your help in making calls on our current justice system. We can and must return to a higher level. The decline in government walks hand-in-hand with the decline in justice. The fervor and constancy of your calls can raise them both.

The scales of justice are out of balance

The scales of justice are no longer in balance. Our very system of justice is in jeopardy. Justice is predicated on certain inalienable principles. If these foundational pillars are ignored, or if the system is treated like a game, then true justice cannot be attained. Justice requires honesty under oath and honor over intrigue and the desire to win. It demands an attitude of not being biased over one of bias. All of these and more were violated in the case of the British au pair *(nanny), who was charged with the murder of a child in her care in 1997.*

A true justice system treats all people equally and maintains fairness in the making of initial charges, the handling of the trial and the handing down of convictions. The American judicial system does not. The rich and powerful can manipulate the system. The poor are its pawns. Some who should be in prison are never charged, and some who are in prison should be freed. The fame a case can bring to a police department, lawyer or judge should not have any influence upon the legal system. But today it does. Televising court cases should not be allowed because it does more to hinder justice and create false heroes than to encourage truth and accurate verdicts.

It would not be that difficult to alter the American system, as its foundations are good and worthy. This would require scrutiny of the current system and a determination to root out all that has encroached upon its original intent.

When the scales of justice are constantly brought to an imbalance, then karma returns to a nation for this evasion of what is right and honorable before God.

I have talked before about the concept of "office." A judge should never be simply a strategic political appointee. Judges should represent nobility within the legal profession and have an integrity all can recognize. Instead, some who wear the robe of judge are an abomination to Portia and to the laws of God-justice for the earth. Others fulfill their offices well and deserve their mantles. These are often burdened in a way they do not comprehend as they help hold a balance against all that is corrupt and out of alignment in the system.

Pray for your justice system and its servants. The tentacles of its dysfunction make everyone vulnerable. May God-justice begin to permeate our country and its courts.

More on the au pair case

The judge in the au pair *case was faced with a karmically weighty dilemma. He knew that there was not adequate evidence to convict the girl. He also knew that emotions were running high and that few judges opt to do what he was contemplating—reversing the verdict. He was not a seeker of fame or fortune. He was a man who believed in the true purpose for which the law was designed. He was not omniscient and thus did not know what had occurred and who, in the end, was guilty. He did know that justice would not be served if the jury's verdict were upheld. He chose on the side of conscience and his true understanding of the law. I can tell you that he passed a significant test.*

I am not permitted to comment on the intricacies of the case of the au pair, *which is much more complex than meets the eye. I can only say that based on the given evidence, the judge acted with courage and a sense of judicial integrity when he overturned what had been handed down.*

My comment is not meant to infer who is guilty or not guilty. We cannot, however, function as a true justice system if we are willing to condemn when there is not adequate or clear cause to do so. The courts, though the center of deeply karmic and emotionally charged issues, are not meant to give their verdicts based on emotion. They are meant to give their verdicts based on the law, facts and clear evidence. They depend on the honesty of witnesses who will take an oath and honor it and not perjure themselves. We must grant to others what we would want for ourselves.

Do you have any comments on people who borrow money and then make no effort to repay it?

I have mentioned several times the importance of your word and your honor. It is the lower self, or not-self, that allows a person to procrastinate and justify not repaying that which was never his or hers to keep. If your fellow men cannot trust you, then God cannot trust you with His light.

What I observe is that people give loans without estab-

lishing clear payment schedules from the onset. It is better to pay something monthly, even if it's only ten dollars or one dollar, than to let months go by without making a payment. This effort toward repayment helps the alchemy of the situation, acting in a way that is similar to the principle of the tithe.

The ultimate sin is to fail to repay the loan and to act nonapologetic, as if nothing is owed to the person who made the loan. Or worse yet—to lie about the situation. You must be honest with yourself. You are accountable for every action you take. Bind all self-justification, intrigue, unreality and disobedience of the law within your psyche.

Loans in and of themselves are not wrong. But the terms of the loan and the attitudes of the recipients and the lenders are critical. Failing to repay a loan may block your abundance for years to come. To be treated with trust and respect, you must live a life that has integrity and honesty as its hallmarks.

CHAPTER EIGHTEEN

Working on the Astral Plane

About the astral plane

Many decent souls are caught in the astral plane[29] due to strong momentums with alcohol and drugs, a lack of forgiveness, committing suicide and/or living lives that were focused on materialism and not on God. And the list goes on.

The astral plane is entwining and entrenching. It seeks to hold you in your momentums. It is devoid of spiritual joy and light, and it grows denser as you descend to even lower levels of it. It is like a prison sentence to be trapped on the astral level.

While working on the astral plane you sometimes encounter souls you have known in this or other lives. Though this is heartrending, even on this level, there is joy in ministering to them and helping them get cut free. The process, however, is not simple. Without the great light in heaven that many of you take for granted, people are slower to change and less clear about the great opportunities in store for them if they are able to advance.

What can you tell us about working on the astral plane?

I must spend a portion of my time attempting to save souls from the astral plane. Working on the astral plane is one of the best ways for us to render service from this side, yet it is not a simple or leisurely task. You may also pray for the opportunity to help free souls from the astral plane. This is a way for you to transmute karma by preaching the Word while you are out of the body in sleep or meditation. You will not be sent on your mission alone. You will always go in the company of angelic bands. But they will not be holding your hand as you preach or minister to individual souls.

Each of us is tied to someone and, most likely, to many individuals who have landed on the astral plane. It may be your duty, or simply your good karma, to minister to the souls you are assigned to help. What makes this work difficult is this: Being on the astral plane can cause people to forget their ties to you and to doubt the true purpose of life. This makes for spiritual warfare at its most intense. You must be deeply attuned to the forces challenging you while holding perfect love for the soul you are attempting to cut free.

I have ministered to people I have known from past lives as well as my present life. My record is far from 100 percent. Being on the astral plane is similar to drug use. Beginners may start out not intending to keep using drugs. They may not even like the drugs. But as the weeks and months continue, their identity aligns more with the drugs and fellow drug users than with their Real Selves and their true friends. What is Real becomes Unreal, and what is Unreal becomes Real to them. Similarly, the astral plane grows on souls. They become more and more accustomed to—even attached to—their surroundings. Just as fellow drug users don't urge them to quit, other souls on their level of the astral plane want to hold them back. The closer souls are to the etheric, the easier they are to reach. Nevertheless, as time passes, even these souls dull to the call of the light.

If you want practice preaching to a hard audience, this is definitely the place to go. Also, you can assist those working to free souls by making daily calls for the setting free of souls of light trapped on the astral plane who are ready to be brought to the etheric.

Rescuing a relative from the astral plane

It is very difficult to minister to souls on the astral plane, as being in the astral dulls the memory body and the ability to remember the light and the true purpose for being. As the years go by and souls cease to seek or search, they become passive. It is far better to reach them soon after they enter the astral plane than years later.

Perhaps the most poignant episode for me was when I had the opportunity to cut my own nephew free. He was on the upper levels of the astral. He was a soul of light who had let alcohol destroy his opportunity to advance spiritually and to *fulfill his dharma. He recognized me right away but needed some counseling to understand where he was and what had trapped him in that astral environment. We cannot take a soul from the astral unless he or she expresses some desire to be free, or without consent on some level.*

Once he was freed from the astral plane, he was taken to the lowest level of the etheric. There he was assigned to a retreat hospital setting where people are sent for the repairing and healing of their finer bodies. Souls who are sent there can begin to receive a course in cosmic law and can be assigned to specific retreats, once enough healing has occurred.

When a soul leaves the astral for the etheric, it is like a patient having bandages removed after months of illness or recovery from surgery. The healing is not instant but gradual. The adjustment is also gradual and takes the compassion and understanding of others. The service rendered in these retreat hospitals is indescribable in its love and patience.

It's very interesting that my husband was able to rescue our nephew from the astral plane, as he had to rescue our nephew many times in this life too. When he was four years old, this boy's father was killed in Korea. After that, my husband became the important male figure in his life. Most of the scrapes he got into were really quite humorous, and he always had "instant karma." Unfortunately, he became an alcoholic later in life. One day when he was drunk he wandered onto a freeway and was killed by a truck. It was a relief to hear that he was being helped after his death, and that for souls who choose the light the healing never ends.

What lessons did you learn from those on the astral plane?

Work on the astral plane is very challenging work. Attempting to help souls on the astral plane is like being a spiritual warrior. Preaching to them can be very difficult. Sometimes I feel as if no one is listening to me, that they have accepted the horrible state they are in. Some still blaspheme God and do not want to hear anything about light, purity, holiness, etc. Others are good souls whose actions have trapped them where they really should not be.

I've seen the ugliness of drug and alcohol abuse. People destroy their lives, hurt others and commit crimes—all for drugs. This can tie them to the astral plane. The entities [30] *that were attached to them when they were alive stay bound to them, and before we can reach a soul, these entities must be fought off. The power to cast out demons, spoken about in the Bible (Matt. 10), is necessary for effective work on the astral plane. You must be fierce against these forces.*

We are given classes in how to work to save souls. We literally rejoice for every soul who moves up, even to the lowest level of the etheric.

I met a man the other day who had been on the astral plane for twenty-four years. He was an alcoholic and had committed suicide. When his family left him, he hit bottom. What was sad was to see that he had been a very fine man, a lawyer with a wife and two children. Through alcohol and neglect, he lost them. And by the time he committed suicide he'd broken many of the Commandments and was a sorry case.

The truth is, however, that he is basically a good soul who in one life made tremendous karma that tied him to the astral plane. I was allowed to tell him of his early self before alcohol entered the picture. I spoke to him of his true destiny and of the goodness of his being. Cutting him free was a very slow process, as the astral plane feeds the sense of worthlessness and despondency to which people have been vulnerable.

It is by love and light, the action of blue-flame protection and the violet flame that we are able to get souls cut free. They must first be ministered to by wisdom and love and then cut free by power. This is truly an amazing work and a privilege. Their fate is so sad, however, that I would pray for you to live in such a way that you are never in danger of ending up on the astral plane.

CHAPTER NINETEEN

The Spiritual Path

The via dolorosa—a Christmas message, 1997

If I were to re-embody knowing what I know now, I would select the path of the via dolorosa *over any other. The pleasures of the world are so deceptive and so entrapping, yet they have no permanence. Anything you suffer for God is like putting money into your spiritual bank account.*

The via dolorosa, *the path of the cross, is not to be feared. Mother Teresa walked this path, yet look at the joy and radiance she and her nuns have exuded! It is in sacrificing for God that you are born to eternal life.*

Many of the children to whom Mother Mary has appeared have been inspired to sacrifice for the salvation of the world. They have not hesitated to do this, as they have under-

stood the need for and the power of such deeds for the treasury of God's work. They have also been repaid a hundredfold for their devotion and obedience.

You can begin this path by examining your life and looking for something you can sacrifice for God. You might give up some free time to pray or to help someone who is ill or emotionally weak. You might fast or give up a pleasurable food to which you are attached. The key is to make a commitment and fulfill it. Each person's life is unique, so one person's sacrifice may be another person's daily routine and not considered a sacrifice. You cannot compare yourself with others. You must be honest with yourself, and you must seek forward movement toward God and toward union with your Holy Christ Self.

A person who is truly on this path may ultimately suffer much in terms of persecution, health demands or sheer and total givingness for God's sake. Your Messenger has suffered more than most of you will ever realize; such is her commitment to the ascended masters and the mission she has been given.

Is this path worthy of your fear? It is the path of the deepest love, the deepest joy and the deepest purity. Only if you fear these qualities should you hesitate to embark on this journey—the journey to the heart of Christ. If you wish to know this heart and have it for your own, then you must begin the walk with your own steps of sacrifice. Each of your steps will be matched with drops of mercy and compassion from the heart of Kuan Yin.[31]

If you truly have the love of Christ, you will suffer to see the desecration of light on this planet. The purity and innocence of our youth is challenged at every turn. The sacredness of life is not revered. The honor of God in government and in our justice system is steadily eroding. This is why Mother Mary weeps. And when the children of God and the sons and daughters of God are awake yet asleep, the saints suffer all the more.

How great is your desire to know God through the gifts of the Holy Spirit? These gifts are bought with a price, and that price involves the sacrificing of the human self for the Christ Self. If Jesus Christ appeared to you and made a substantial request of your time, energy and abundance, would you turn him down? Or would you obey? Your answer has a lot to do with your faith and the depth of your commitment to spiritual progress, as well as your attunement with the Word. Pray to be available to answer the call of God whenever and wherever it comes.

You may wonder why this is what I want to share with you on Christmas. It is precisely because it is Christmas that I have talked about the via dolorosa. Members of the holy family followed this path in their own ways, starting with Anna and Joachim, who sacrificed to be worthy to give birth to Mary. Then Mary sacrificed as a young woman in preparation for her parenting of Jesus. She was asked time and again to sacrifice the ways of human motherhood in order to honor the mission of her son. Joseph lived a sacrificial life for God before he was selected to be the father of Jesus. Jesus himself sacrificed much just to come into embodiment and to fulfill a demanding mission that asked much of him at every turn.

Those who walk and talk with God would know that

this is the Christmas story. Out of much love and sacrifice the Christ is born.

Becoming the Christ

There comes a point on the path of every disciple when he must choose whom he will serve—God or mammon. The test comes when the aspirant has progressed and made many positive changes within and without, has done many novenas and has purified his life. The fact is, however, that the ties, both subtle and obvious, to the world of mammon remain.

The final turning point is when the person truly wants God—wants the Holy Spirit—above all else. Many never achieve this last step. This is what distinguishes the saints from noble and decent aspirants. These vital years call for at least some among you to want your Christhood and the sacrifice it will entail above all else. Unlike some life choices, this is one that you will never regret. However, it is not for the faint of heart.

When your goals are absolutely clear and your sails are set for the kingdom of God, all is attainable and the sufferings of the world can be borne. The more that you give to God, the more you are given. As with all things of the Spirit, this is a perfect equation.

Only you can make the final decision regarding how far up the mountain you will ascend. It is between your soul and God. Pray for God-desire and strength and clarity of purpose. Your prayers will be answered if they are earnest and heartfelt.

On drawing down ideas from the etheric plane

The etheric plane is composed of several levels and also of retreats that specialize in specific fields such as healing, science and art or love. Souls ultimately end up at a retreat that represents their specialization of service over lifetimes. Creative work that emphasizes these fields of study continues on the etheric levels. This is why some people have ideas come to them during sleep, after they have traveled to an etheric retreat. Others draw down ideas from their own treasure house or Causal Body that they have built over lifetimes.

Many ideas that could transform the earth are waiting to be released, but earth is not prepared. In fact, in many ways it is dangerously unprepared. The emergence of a golden age is not guaranteed. It depends largely on those in embodiment—not on those in the etheric realm.

Unfortunately, I observe on earth the misuse of every chakra and much corruption, often in high places. Scientists are daily realizing new vistas of possibility through genetic research and other areas. Man is not ready to make judgments on all that is being brought forward. Some discoveries may be worthy vehicles of great healing. Others may stand as the abomination where it ought not to be.[32] *Pray about all things that come to your attention. God-direction and God-solutions are available for everything, but you must make the calls.*[33]

212 Messages from Heaven

Upon hearing of Mother Teresa's death, can you say anything about her? We know you always loved and respected her.

Mother Teresa was in every way a saint. She received her calling from the masters at inner levels, and she fulfilled it beyond expectations. Some writers with little discernment and great ego have insinuated that Mother Teresa should have changed political policies for the poor, or that she was wrong to have brought in the money she did for her missions. God is not pleased with these comments, as they come from people attempting to sit in judgment where they have no place and no mantle.

Each person's calling is unique. Mother Teresa was to serve the poorest of the poor. She did this with such profound love and awareness of the dignity of each soul that she actually bought extra time for this planet. She saw the Christ in everyone. Her very presence helped others to want to do better, to give more and to serve more. Her presence was a healing force in and of itself. Her work was spiritually practical, but it also had great spiritual depth. She did not just talk the talk; she walked the walk. She lived the teachings of Christ.

Mother Teresa never sought any of the fame that came to her. In fact, it caused her spiritual angst and physical pain. The fame was truly Christ's and not hers. She understood this, but those covering her story could not fully comprehend it. Abundance came to her missions, but this is the way of spiritual alchemy. She was God's vessel. As she once said, "I am just a pencil in the Lord's hand." God provides abundance when it is necessary to the work of a saint. She was free of *greed, hatred, covetousness and other earthly foibles. Her desire was to save souls and serve the poor. This she did magnificently.*

Though she was a Catholic through and through, Mother Teresa honored the ways of all that she met. She condemned no one for his or her spiritual persuasion, and she served all who were sent her way. There are great lessons in this.

There is a reason that Mother Teresa's home was in India. She represented the Mother flame and India came to honor her as the Mother.

Heaven was waiting for her arrival. Her life was a cause for celebration in the etheric realm. Indeed, the words "well done" echoed through our halls, and we all felt joy in her accomplishments. This daughter of God understood joy as few have known it.

It is important to note that her calling did not come easily or simply at first; very few do. Mother Teresa prayed without ceasing and studied to internalize the deepest meaning of Christ's teaching. She was guided throughout her mission because of the purity of her intent and her dedication to the will of God. Her evolution to saint, however, was a path and a process. The greatest pity will be if others do not realize that this path is open to all who seek it with the fervor and commitment that she modeled.

Which gift of the Holy Spirit should we pray for first?

Probably the most important gift of the Holy Spirit to pray for is discernment. Without discernment, the seeker is vulnerable to be moved hither and thither and to potentially misuse other gifts or to not recognize the true teachings from the false.

With discernment you know the vibration of truth and nontruth, good and evil, purity and impurity, holiness and the impostors of holiness. You can pick up a book and know to what degree it contains truth.

Many seekers who lack discernment are drawn to books and individuals that are not of the light or, at best, not of the highest vibration. It should be a daily practice to ask for this holy gift. I myself lacked it in a certain way in that I was drawn in or fooled by certain ads and certain politicians because they were saying what I wanted to hear.

On the heart

The complexity of each lifestream, as a composite of the choices he or she has made over the centuries, is vast. It is such a waste of time, and also spiritual misconduct, to sit in the seat of the accuser of your brethren. The seemingly ornery one may be much closer to Christhood than the one who appears polite and kind on the outer. The heart is at the core of everything, and God alone is the discerner of our hearts.

If you rarely experience the fire in your heart, I heartily recommend Saint Germain's Heart Meditations.[34] You must get past what is blocking your heart. Often people mistake human efficiency—a strong intellect and the ability to follow the rules—for good discipleship. But discipleship without heart breeds a mechanical mentality instead of true discipleship. It is like a Montana winter with no heat.

Hearts can be blocked for a myriad of reasons. Do not

condemn yourself or assume the worst if you do not feel your heart flame. On the other hand, recognize that there is work to be done. Some people close off their hearts due to traumas or painful events they cannot handle. Others are greedy, or their egos cause them to be self-centered, forgetting the plights of others. We are our brother's keepers; we do bear one another's burdens. Your very presence should be a refuge for those who seek God's love. This cannot occur without attention to the heart.

For a good visualization, see the violet flame transmuting all your hardness of heart and all blocks to the balance of your heart.

On discouragement

There is no more subtle force than discouragement. I say this because few people view discouragement as spiritually or emotionally dangerous. Yet this energy can be used by the forces of evil to cause people to doubt their God and to abandon their true purpose.

The path to union with the Holy Spirit is not a walk in the park. It requires a willingness to enter the refiner's fire, which intensifies as you attain to greater heights on the path. By its very nature this fire brings challenge to your door. It finds ways to help you realize your dependency on God and your I AM Presence. When you are in the succor of human and physical comfort, this is not likely to occur. We all need prodding. If even Jesus felt moments of abandonment, how much greater may be our need to feel alone and without purpose. This period is always shortened for the soul who acknowledges God's love and presence and accepts with grace the challenge that is before her. It's when discouragement is allowed to fester and prevail that the soul loses momentum and prolongs the test and the agony.

Discouragement is the antithesis of the abundant consciousness. It blocks gratitude and alchemy. Discouraged people are often blinded to what they do have and what they have received because they are so focused on wanting one event, person or state of being that they can no longer see what they have already been given.

On accountability

I must speak to you about accountability. It is an aspect of the human condition and the lower self to wish to forget that which the soul knows in her deepest part—her "heart of hearts." It is the way of the dweller, along with the temptations of Satan, to pull us from our spiritual moorings and roots and to attract us to the subtle or not-so-subtle enticements of this world.

Watching from the other side, I witness many dear souls who are trapped in an ongoing dance that takes them back and forth between divine purpose and human desire. The more attainment the soul has, the less obvious are the temptations that pull her away from God's will. But nevertheless they are there.

As long as one speck of an Achilles' heel remains, the soul is vulnerable. This is why the masters urge their students to be wise concerning their psychology and honest about their desires. Only by facing ourselves and our momentums can we eventually be freed. I speak from experience, as many aspects of my consciousness left me vulnerable, and I was not always attuned to or wise about those parts of myself.

Many times other people are used to bring to our doorstep the very circumstances to which we are vulnerable. The test is to recognize the serpent no matter what its disguise and to challenge the temptation. Biblically we know that some of the greatest tests may come from those of our "own household." (Matt. 10:36) Household can mean our own community members, ourselves or those with whom we live or are related. This doesn't mean that those souls are not kind of heart or strong lightbearers. It simply means that the forces of evil are cunning; they will place challenge where we least expect it. They will use whatever they can, whenever they can.

Where does accountability come into play, you ask? We are not pawns of a predetermined destiny. We have opportunity and free will. All that we have been taught spiritually on the outer, and all the tutoring of our souls on the inner, are both gifts and obligations. With knowledge and wisdom comes responsibility.

What I observe, and what I have been shown, is man's proclivity to repeat similar errors from cycle to cycle. The prophets have an unenviable job. Unless they repeat something daily, people tend to forget it or decide that it no longer applies. They wish to make merry and to seek comfort at all levels. They become experts in self-justification. They negotiate with God when they should be seeking to heed His words with gratitude.

Many adults behave like children who say things like, "Susie's parents let her do this, and so do Nora's. So why can't I?" Similarly, adults say to themselves, "Harry moved, then stopped his spiritual practice, and he's doing better than I am. Why shouldn't I do the same thing?" Or, "I've sacrificed *financially and personally to follow this path, and my cousin Bob has never sacrificed. But he has much more to show for those years, and he's a happy man with a nice family."* We can never judge another person's path or attainment. We must walk our own path and seek constant communion with God's purpose for our lives. We are accountable for what we have been shown and what we have learned spiritually. The teachings of God's emissaries are intended to raise us up to our Higher Selves. They are not meant to appease our lower selves or our human whims or desires.

Yes, there is mercy and there is forgiveness. But it is far better to listen to what you know and obey than to have to learn everything the hard way by trial and error. The more precarious the times such as we are now experiencing, the more important it is to listen to what we know instead of being like children, wanting to bask in the sunshine and be entertained while destiny calls us elsewhere.

Accountability is a prime concept about which we are tutored in the etheric realms. One way or another, every jot and tittle must be balanced. When people deny this lesson, they make choices they later regret, and regret is one of the worst punishments we can place on ourselves. Regret implies that we are suffering over a lost opportunity—something we could have done but chose not to do. I wish to spare you from this.

The fire of the heart

People tend to beg God for events to go the way they desire. Yet so many events are determined by the equation of effort toward spiritual progress and by the expansion of the heart. *More can be granted to those who are the becomers than to those who remain the dabblers or the "on-again, off-again" students. Commitment to holy purpose counts for much in heaven, just as commitment and dependability matter on the earth plane.*

What is the quality of the wood—or works—that you place on the fire of your heart? How often do you tend this fire? Does it heat your temple or does it wax strong and weak as your attention goes hither and yon? What would it take for you to see the garnering of the fire of your heart as part of your divine labor?

The practice of the presence of God and the tending of the fire of the heart are paramount to your progress. May you seek them both with joy and gratitude.

The missing link

I would like to talk to you about the missing link. As I have observed and studied students on the path, I have seen that for many, what appears to be the missing part of the equation is an understanding of how to balance livelihood, family and a desire to progress spiritually. In reality the missing component is a true desire to become the Christ above all else.

If you really seek the ultimate goal, the masters have provided numerous teachings on how to achieve it. The truth has been highlighted in every true path to God. When the student is ready and the desire to become the Christ is not distant, or strong one hour and weak the next, all will fall into place.

I did not have this as my ultimate goal when I was in embodiment. I did wish to serve God and to serve others for

God. I did want to be a "good person." These were lawful desires, and they helped me to progress. They were, however, short of the mark. So much of what I truly sought was only attainable through becoming one with the Christ Self. Yes, the path seems demanding. But we actually put up with so much more by postponing the freedom and clarity that will come with the path of Christhood.

So many people postpone their own progress by debating about whether others are making right decisions. Or they become bothered or hurt by the treatment of a fellow seeker on the path. There is not one person—not one saint—who has not experienced difficult moments with fellow seekers, their spiritual teachers or their families. This is part and parcel of being on a genuine spiritual path. It would be better to focus on how to be of more service, how to grow in compassion and mercy toward life, and how to walk in imitation of Christ.

People are far more apt to rise up spiritually if we hold the immaculate concept for them than if we scrutinize, analyze and debate every quality of their beings.

Many of you are close to truly desiring your Christhood. Try to discover what impediment keeps you from the full desire. Are you at peace with this impediment, or do you want to be one-pointed in your pursuit?

Right now some of you want to find a marriage partner, pursue a college degree, have financial security or buy or build a home more than you want to advance spiritually. These are all lawful desires. But it is possible to attain them and not put your Christhood in second or third place. The question is one of dharma. Each soul has different things to achieve in *order to fulfill the call of dharma. In your deepest heart you know whether God is first or second on your list of pursuits. When the highest is allowed to drive all other parts of your life, everything you are meant to have will fall into place.*

Understanding the Teacher or Guru

The history of the rebellion of the lightbearers fills more volumes than we may realize. To understand the living Teacher, particularly for the Western mind, is challenging. The living Teacher may make some grievous errors, but the point is that the Teacher has the mantle, the sponsorship of God.

As long as the vibration of the teaching is pure, you can know that God is with the prophet. The Guru may accept wrong advice. The Teacher may allow people who are not the best choice to be in positions of management and seeming power. The Guru can make karma. Your Teacher has never claimed otherwise. She has never set herself apart from all others, but she has proclaimed the mantle of Messenger because she does bear this.

People tend to project on the Guru all that is unresolved in their own psychology. Lightbearers have often doubted their Teacher, particularly when the message was hard or the years passed and the demands continued. We seem to resist the disciplined love that the path takes.

The West does not understand the concept of the path. In the Eastern religions people understand the importance of the Teacher and the Teaching as guideposts to God and to what is one's true identity.

Mother Mary's rosary creates a giant chalice of light

The rosary has waned in popularity. It has received little understanding outside of the Catholic Church and Church Universal and Triumphant. It was intended to be a vehicle of intercession for all Christian lightbearers and others who understood its power and purpose. The rosary, when given with regularity and purity of heart, helps to ignite the flame within. Each rosary offered with the fervor of a sincere supplicant is added to a giant chalice of light specifically maintained by the rosary. The rosary not only benefits the one who prays it; it also helps to hold a significant balance for the planet.

Through the centuries, dispensations have been granted that offered lightbearers a means to multiply and magnify their prayers. The rosary is a dispensation of great import. It is neither meant to go in and out of fashion, nor is it to be viewed as "old fashioned" by the most recent generations. It is a gift to the lightbearers—a method of accelerating light in their lives—and for the planet. It is not meant for vain repetition, but rather to be a meditation on Christ's life and a prayer of the heart. It remains one of the best ways to pray for the healing of someone you love. The prayer of consecration that is given in your church following the rosary is of great importance. It allows an interchange between the country or person being consecrated and the power of the Immaculate Heart of Mary and it helps fulfill the request of Mother Mary at Fátima that Russia be consecrated to her.

I have given my own witness to the rosary in several of my writings. I had just finished a novena to the rosary before

*my death. I completed it in the hospital despite how weak I was
feeling, as I had given my word that I would do this. Upon
my transition both the dedication to my promise and the
prayers themselves were honored.*

*To neglect the rosary is to neglect Mother Mary and her
fiery heart that longs to save each and every one of us. In giving the rosary, seek to unite with her Immaculate Heart and
seek to increase the fire in your own heart. I guarantee that it
will change your life.*

We were asked to do the rosary immediately after this message was given. And we were asked to place a picture of Mother
Mary showing her Immaculate Heart next to us while giving the
rosary.

Outsmarting the fallen angels

*I am telling less about myself than I did in the begin-
ning. I am so aware that this will be my final dispensation. I
feel an urgency to help people recognize the signs of the times.
I am not instructed as to what I must say. I am, however,
limited in specific ways as to what I can share.*

*I have manifested many other faults in my embodiments
that I could have shared. I have also witnessed so many beautiful and amazing events on this side. However, I believe that
my greatest opportunity is to urge you to see what you have,
where the planet is headed without intervention, and how you
can make a difference.*

*I note that many of you are surprised when certain dif-
ficult events occur; yet you have diligently given your decrees or
prayers on the specific day that you encountered the opposition.*

This can happen for a number of reasons. First, you need as much specificity as possible in your calls. If you are working on a new project or hoping for a certain job, every aspect of it must be protected. Decrees and prayers should not be global and nonspecific. They need to be as precise as you can make them. Second, sometimes what looks like opposition may actually be an act of mercy. Karmically, something much worse may have been due. Finally, all important events are opposed by the fallen ones. Light will always prevail, but it is often necessary for the battle to be fought. The fallen ones do not vacation. They are ever hopeful to defeat the light through the forces of discouragement, confusion, temptation, lack of self-worth, lack of forgiveness, anger and gossip. They love to trap people in their karma, as they know that, without these subtle and not-so-subtle manipulations, Light will always be the victor. The solution is to outsmart them with faith, hope, purity, love, honor, obedience, forgiveness and all of the God-qualities.

Those who have had the faith of a child—with unequivocal trust in God to solve all things—have always persevered and prevailed.

Examine your areas of vulnerability and work to overcome them. Be diligent in your daily calls to protect all aspects of your comings and goings and those of your loved ones. Penetrating light is the alchemical key.

The true spirit of service

I wish to speak about service unto the Lord. Many feign service out of an obligation or a need to appear good before men. This is not true service. True service is a state of being, a sense that you are born to serve. It is a part of your very nature, and you need it for the nourishment of your soul and the beating of your heart. True service is a joy. We ask God for so much, and we depend on God for His grace and His mercy. God asks of us the genuine service of our hearts. When you serve with your heart, others feel it and are drawn and connected to you by the purity of your motive.

The spirit of service comes naturally to some. But in most people it must be rekindled or developed. Children must be given meaningful opportunities to serve in the community, the church and the home, and to reach others within the worldwide community. Service engenders meaning, self-esteem, responsibility and honor in young people as they are forming their identities in this lifetime. Often we need the people we serve more than they need us. We should thank God for every opportunity that we are given to serve.

Today is Thanksgiving, a day of gratitude unto God for the opportunity of life and the beauty that is ours to claim.

Jesus lived a life of service. Study his life for an understanding of the flame of service. When you make your transition, you will be grateful beyond words for every genuine, self-less act of service that you have performed. It is true that on the etheric plane you meet souls whom you have served, sometimes many lifetimes ago, who stop to thank you because they are aware of the significance of your service to their spiritual progress.

The worst deterrent to service is self-absorption. There are people who feel that their pain is too deep or their problems too large to give any attention to the needs of others. Beware of these states of consciousness overcoming you. Just the slightest act of love toward someone else might help your own healing or your capacity to endure. Other people are too absorbed in their jobs or their moneymaking to notice those around them. No life is complete without service, and no condition is an excuse for a person to cease to think of the well-being of others.

Some appoint themselves to sit in the seat of the accuser as critic of some of God's best servants. Every time you condemn another, you condemn yourself in some way. Consider the services you have rendered this past week. What has motivated your service? Whom are you serving?

Internalizing the Word

My strongest observation of late is that so few people understand the internalization of the Word. To internalize the Word you must actually become it. The teachings of the ascended masters cannot be separate from your being. They are not like a book to be placed on the shelf and referred to from time to time. They are living. They are light. They are the open door to your spiritual path and your overcoming.

Can you imagine the patience of the ascended hosts when they have seen some of us fail to comprehend what it means to internalize the most important truths lifetime after lifetime? Can you imagine their patience as they have had to watch certain momentums of gossip, criticism, unworthiness, fear and pride recur century after century? It is interesting to contemplate why we hold on to a momentum such as criticism for lifetimes. How is it serving us? What does it allow us to accomplish? Who is in control when we are critical or gossiping?

Even when the Messenger or the ascended masters give teachings on these momentums, many fail to see their own culpability. Karma is blinding, but we do not have to remain in this state.

The masters have said a great deal about pride. Pride can be blatant, but in many it is subtle yet deadly. Remember that the masters have stated that it is pride that keeps us feeling that we are not worthy of God's forgiveness. It is pride that makes us feel that we must do everything ourselves without accepting the help of others.

I was famous for thinking that I had to be in charge and lift the heaviest box or object or do the hardest part of a manual job. I just wanted to be helpful, or so I thought. But in reality I never considered the other person's need to help or the reality of my own physical stamina. I was prideful of my ability to be on par with someone half my age. I did not see this or admit it to myself, but I do now.

Self-justification has its roots in pride. It must also be watched as a dangerous momentum. At its worst level, it can be used to justify the vilest actions. Only the will of God is justified. Seek that will.

CHAPTER TWENTY

Teachings on the Path

Mother Mary

Mother Mary, our tireless Mother, works day and night to awaken her children. She has continued to believe in her children when others might have abandoned hope.

Mother Mary serves in many roles. She is an intercessor and mediatrix. She is a healer, counselor and bearer of miracles. Her messages bring hope, guidance, chastisement and warning. Though they may appear simple, if we heed them they will transform the world and spare people much pain. The themes of her appearances have included many repeated requests. She asks that we seek peace in our hearts, which comes through forgiving others and ourselves. The path to this peace is through divine love.

The spiritual practices she advocates are praying, giving the rosary and fasting regularly. She calls us to sacrifice now on behalf of a better future. She chastises greed, dishonesty and placing materialism above God as well as all forms of selfishness and self-love. She calls herself the "Mother of All Nations." She does not want to be relegated to Catholics alone, for she serves in the flame of the Mother all who seek her counsel and love.

What has kept her messages from being received by the broader Christian church? Can people of God not overcome their attachment to faulty doctrine to recognize an emissary of God and of his son Jesus Christ? It's time for Mother Mary to be understood in the broader sense of her role, not just inserted into the local church nativity play at Christmas.

What I have learned since my transition is how much Mother Mary was a pillar of light and strength after the ascension of Jesus. She is, in many ways, the Mother of our Christian dispensation. Though she was devout, modest and humble, her role and impact were extraordinary. Jesus confided many things to her, and after his ascension she understood in a deeper way his mission and the work that needed to be done to secure the foundation of the Piscean Age. As we know from the Bible, Mother Mary held many truths in her heart. (Luke 2:19) This means that she heard the inner teachings of God and his angels and she followed them.

She has typically selected the humble and less fortunate (in a worldly sense) to receive her messages. She knows that the pride of the haughty and the materialism of the rich can be blocks to obedience, purity and a willingness to look foolish before mankind on behalf of God.

As I stated earlier, Mother Mary greeted me as I made my transition from earth to the etheric realm. For me the experience was like being in the presence of the essence of divine love, beauty and healing. Imagine when this occurs to someone who is to remain in embodiment! It creates an indelible record—a record more powerful than anything the person has ever experienced. This record is tangible and accessible, like words of living fire. This is why those who receive her messages can retain them, and those who see her during the same apparition describe precisely the same scene and details.

Mother Mary has healed countless numbers. She has overshadowed more projects of merit and been at more rosary groups than people will ever realize.

When one's twin flame is ascended

Ascended twin flames cannot interfere with the free will of their counterparts who are still in embodiment. They can make calls and they do hold a balance, but they cannot protect the one in embodiment from returning karma. Every ascended being holds a desire in his heart for the victory of the light-bearers. The twin flame longs for the return and the victory of the divine complement, but not in any human sense.

The one in embodiment may feel a profound loneliness, a sense that something cannot be found on this earth. This one can be happily married and still sense that something intangible is missing. The solution is to become the Christ, to fulfill your dharma. For every act of good and love you render others, you serve your twin flame as well. It is lawful to make *calls for your twin flame, and if you know that he or she is ascended, you can regularly call on assistance from the etheric realms.*

Everyone seems to search for a twin flame in embodiment. It is important to remember that many twin flames are ascended, waiting for their divine counterparts to join them. The best favor you can offer your twin flame is your willingness to face and conquer your human self. It is this synthetic self that has kept you apart or brought you together, only to pull you apart again.

There are those who sacrifice the path while they think they are searching for their twin flame. The twin flame is far more apt to find you or appear to you if you place the path before all else.

There are marvelous souls with whom some of you have missions or excellent karma. The one you are drawn to may not be your twin flame, but you can love and honor him or her as you would your twin flame.

Personally, I can show no greater love for my twin flame than to fulfill the current mission I have been given. This knowledge helps me to move forward as quickly as I can. Yet this is what I would need to do whether my twin flame were advancing or going backward on the path.

If your twin flame is ascended, you are never alone. Though humanly separated, you are spiritually connected. Seek to know the spiritual connection and the aloneness will fade.

We asked the following question about Patricia Johnson, a member of our community who was loved by all who knew her.

As a minister she performed many weddings and was always counseling and helping people. She became very ill when she was in her sixties and fought death valiantly over a period of several years. Most people didn't know how much she suffered at times. On the day she finally left her body, we all knew that something special had happened. The whole sky over our valley became covered with clouds of a glorious golden pink color. Shortly thereafter the Messenger announced that Patricia would be making her ascension and that she wanted us all to participate in the ceremony that would take place about a month later.

Is there anything you'd like to say about Patricia Johnson's ascension?

Patricia Johnson's life has lessons for all. People should study the lives of those who ascend.

Patricia was very approachable. In many ways she lived by Saint Francis' prayer. She preferred to console rather than to seek consolation. Her focus was not on what she could obtain for herself, but rather what she could give to others. She was a good mother and shared the Mother flame with all she met.

Patricia was very practical. There was little unreality within her. She had a deep reverence for the will of God and sought to honor it in all she did. She understood the role of spiritual obedience and became concerned if something seemed out of alignment with her understanding of the law.

Perhaps most importantly, she knew that when love is missing, being angry with or judging a person will not change things. Rather, attempting to supply the missing love is the ultimate key to its emergence. The best way to learn of love is to experience true love from the heart of another. To be punished or accused for lacking love will never bring about the transformation that love itself can provide.

Those who talked at Patricia's memorial service did not begin to represent the literal multitude who were touched by her in significant ways—ways that were lasting and spiritually transforming. Her actions left a positive record with most people she encountered, a record they can draw on and be inspired by until their own transitions.

Patricia was also very organized. It is a God-quality to be organized. Organization allows everything to flow without interruption or delay. A God-oriented organizer is open to suggestions for change and creativity. Organization provides a framework whereby progress can more easily occur than it can in an atmosphere of constant chaos. Believe me, there is an order to the etheric retreats. It is an order based on truth and pure knowledge. It is an order that allows for transcendence. Therefore, it remains fluid yet precise.

Patricia was also a cleaner par excellence, but this is not unusual for those on purity's ray. What is tolerable to others is not acceptable to those who know the true vibration of purity. They must recreate and establish it everywhere they go.

Though she suffered greatly in the flesh, Patricia bore this nobly. Few know the degree of her suffering, as she kept much to herself.

Patricia is one who has triumphed, and there are clues in her life for everyone who walks the path of the ascended masters on earth. Now that she has overcome, she has returned to her home and to her twin flame.

If you were to take your leave of earth today, what would others say of you? What example would you have left for others? It is in day-to-day living, and in the overcoming of the obstacles that are set in your path, that so much of your life is determined. Treasure the hours that you are given, and assess your use of those hours.

I lived to be eighty. My life seemed in many ways like the twinkling of an eye. The years pass quickly and opportunities occur daily. Do not let your psychology keep you from the progress you are meant to achieve. Right decisions are celebrated in heaven; they are light. Faulty decisions are a baggage, a burden that can be transmuted. Make your decisions count for light.

On the day of Patricia's ascension, members of our church attended a service during which we sang songs and did decrees and prayers for the victory of her soul. The Messenger described the service as it was taking place in the etheric ascension temple over the beautiful ancient temple ruin at Luxor, Egypt. We felt as if we were really there. Later we asked my husband if he had also attended the ceremony.

About the ascension ceremony

Patricia Johnson's ascension ceremony has been magnificent, regal, etheric and victorious thus far. The entire ceremony will last the equivalent of several days, so I am sharing this with you from the midst of the ceremony at Luxor.

Many of us—both ascended and unascended beings—have come from other retreats. We are all dressed in white.

Those of us who are unascended are wearing colored strips of cloth around the back of our necks and down each side in the color of the ray of our retreats. Mine, of course, is violet.

Patricia's ceremony has been more public than most. It has been a gift from her to all of you in the hope that the ascension might seem more attainable and more desirable to everyone on the path.

Those of you who knew Patricia might not recognize her now. She is taller, with long, flowing, reddish hair. She is radiant. The tone of the ceremony is hard to describe. We are all one in concentrating on the final acceleration and ascension of this soul. The retreat at Luxor is not disturbed by thoughts of curiosity, envy, gossip or any negative vibration. It is absolutely pure. The music accelerates the consciousness of all who are here.

I feel that I have also been transformed in some way by this ceremony, as I know many of you who have joined in the ceremony have felt uplifted in significant ways.

Conclusion

The nature of the etheric octave

Remember that God stated that he created man in his own image and then he expected man to create a heaven on earth. For a substantial period of time this did occur. The stories of Lemuria and Atlantis relate to this time. However, when man "fell," things changed and life on earth became arduous and quite dense.

The etheric realm is like heavenly cities which don't have the restrictions of time and space like we do on earth. God is transcendent and so is all of his creation, including the angelic realm and souls evolving.

Those of us who reside in the etheric have tasks to perform, often on behalf of planet earth or other systems where there is life. We have classes and lessons to learn. We have music, libraries, meeting halls, places of worship and more. The etheric realm is filled with activity, all for a holy purpose, all in honor of the light and our creators. It is a loving environment blessed by harmony, wisdom and the power of God.

We who have not ascended but still have the opportunity to ascend from this level have a more prescribed routine and clear goals for what we need to accomplish in order to ascend. We live in a specific part of Saint Germain's retreat. We are not shown everything that takes place here. What I have seen would amaze you—but not if you really contemplated the miraculous nature of God.

As I have stated earlier, there are levels to the etheric. Those who are on the lowest levels of the etheric are mainly souls who will definitely re-embody. The work that they do and the nature of their retreats is somewhat different but the basic principles still hold true. We all serve on the astral realm to cut souls free. We all study for our own evolution and we all have specific missions on behalf of embodied life. Our bodies are etheric and yet they have form and dimension.

Everyone here who has not ascended has a deep awareness of the gift of embodiment. Remember to face the lessons being placed before you, as each obstacle that you overcome will be a cause for rejoicing when you get to this side. Life on earth presents opportunities to face everything you need to grow and transcend.

The longer I am at the retreat of Saint Germain, the more difficult it is for me to convey Saint Germain's incredible spiritual stature. His concern for his flock is beyond anything we think of as compassion or parental love. I am transformed regularly just by his presence. Words are not necessary, and yet when he does speak, it has an authority, a wisdom and a joy that is the embodiment of all that he is. Listening to him gives meaning to the concept of The Word.

This book will fulfill the task I was assigned by order and permission of the ascended masters. I will be deeply gratified if many of you have grown or gained spiritual insights from reading this book. I have been as honest as I could be about my own past in the hope that you might do better as you learn from my mistakes. I have also tried to point out some of the things I did that helped me to advance.

I have used this opportunity to comment on broad issues of spiritual importance. Everything I have selected is based on my observations of lightbearers and on areas in their lives which, if changed, could help them succeed spiritually.

As the dispensation comes to a close, I must tell you that this opportunity has been for me the privilege of lifetimes. I am in awe of the ascended master's love for each of you and their desire to see you succeed. I have received special tutoring for this mission. A number of ascended masters have spoken with me, both to educate me and to ask my opinions concerning current conditions on the planet where I was so recently embodied. I urge you to call on the masters, to bond with them and ultimately to become one with them.

There are many more things I could have shared about the etheric realm and about further lessons I have learned since I arrived here. However, this was not the mission of this dispensation. All that I was supposed to convey has been given, along with some additional answers to questions you posed that I have been permitted to answer.

I pray that all who read this will find some pearl that can help them move forward on the path. I am eternally grateful for each person who is led to this book and will read it. May you know God's deepest blessings and guidance as you journey homeward.

Notes

1. Etheric retreats are cities of light that exist in the highest dimension of matter, called the etheric plane. The etheric plane is "experienced through the senses of the soul in a dimension and a consciousness beyond physical awareness." *Saint Germain On Alchemy: Formulas for Self-Transformation*, recorded by Mark L. Prophet and Elizabeth Clare Prophet (Corwin Springs, Mont.: Summit University Press, 1993), p. 402.

2. A lightbearer is one who bears the light of the Christ and carries the responsibility for Christhood in himself and others by defending the truth and honor of God (*Saint Germain On Alchemy*, p. 418).

3. The Causal Body "surrounds the individual I AM presence and contains the records of man's good works—all of God's energy which he has qualified positively in this life and in past lives." (Annice Booth, *The Path to Your Ascension*, [Corwin Springs, Mont.: Summit University Press, 1999], p. 95.) It is the "storehouse of every good and perfect thing that is part of our true identity." (*Saint Germain On Alchemy*, p. 370.)

4. Elizabeth Clare Prophet, *Violet Flame to Heal Body, Mind & Soul* (Corwin Springs, Mont.: Summit University Press, 1997), p. 91.

5. Elizabeth Clare Prophet, *Saint Germain On Prophecy: Coming World Changes*, (Corwin Springs, Mont.: Summit University Press, 1986), p. 29.

6. See Isabel Cooper Oakley, *Le Comte de Saint Germain* (London: Theosophical Publishing House, 1927).

7. *Saint Germain On Alchemy*, p. xxix.

8. Ibid., p. xxix.

9. Oakley, *Le Comte de Saint Germain*.

10. *Saint Germain On Alchemy.*

11. For more information about the ascension, see Booth, *The Path to Your Ascension.*

12. For a better understanding of alchemy, see *Saint Germain On Alchemy.*

13. See *Head, Heart and Hand Decrees* released by Elizabeth Clare Prophet (Corwin Springs, Mont.: Church Universal and Triumphant, 1998), p. 8.

14. See Elizabeth Clare Prophet, *Reincarnation: The Missing Link in Christianity* (Corwin Springs, Mont.: Summit University Press, 1997).

15. See Mark L. Prophet and Elizabeth Clare Prophet, *The Lost Teachings of Jesus,* Books 1–4 (Corwin Springs, Mont.: Summit University Press, 1986).

16. *The History of The Summit Lighthouse,* a pamphlet published in 1994 by Church Universal and Triumphant (Corwin Springs, Mont.)

17. *Saint Germain On Alchemy,* pp. 415–16.

18. *Webster's Ninth New Collegiate Dictionary* (Springfield, Mass.: Merriam-Webster, 1987), s.v. "dharma."

19. See *Invocations to the Hierarchy of the Ruby Ray* through the Messenger Elizabeth Clare Prophet (Corwin Springs, Mont.: Church Universal and Triumphant, 1998).

20. In the sense of an interconnected pattern of spiritual relationships.

21. There have been four dispensations of the ascended masters in the last one hundred and fifty years: 1) The Theosophical Society through Helena P. Blavatsky; 2) the Agni Yoga Society through Nicholas and Helena Roerich; 3) the I AM Movement through Guy and Edna Ballard and 4) The Summit Lighthouse and Church Universal and Triumphant through Mark L. and Elizabeth Clare Prophet. (*Saint Germain On Alchemy,* p. xxix.)

22. See *Saint Germain On Alchemy.*

23. For more information on community, see M. Scott Peck, *A Different Drum: Community Making and Peace* (New York: Simon & Schuster, 1987).

24. Ibid.

25. For more information on paradigm shifts, see Joel A. Barker, *Paradigms: The Business of Discovering the Future* (New York: HarperBusiness, 1993).

26. *Saint Germain On Alchemy.*

27. Ibid., pp. 3–48.

28. Ibid.

29. The astral plane is the "repository of the collective thought/feeling patterns, conscious and unconscious, of mankind." It exists in a "frequency of time and space beyond the physical yet below the mental, corresponding with the emotional body of man and the collective unconscious of the race." But that emotional level has been "muddied by impure human thought and feeling," and on it we find the souls of people who have been caught in its negativity. They are trapped there until their own desire for something higher takes them out of that level or they are rescued. The Catholic and Episcopal tradition of Jesus preaching to the souls in hell is a type of rescue. (*Saint Germain On Alchemy*, pp. 362–63)

30. Entities may be demons or discarnate earthbound spirits.

31. Kuan Yin ascended thousands of years ago and is known as the Goddess of Mercy and the Divine Mother of the East. She is venerated in China, Japan and other Asian countries. See *Saint Germain On Alchemy*, p. 415.

32. Mark:13:14 KJV. "But when ye shall see the abomination of desolation, spoken of by Daniel the prophet, standing where it ought not, (let him that readeth understand), then let them that be in Judæa flee to the mountains."

33. The angels are not allowed to intercede on mankind's behalf unless they are asked.

34. Available on audiotape from Summit University Press, PO Box 5000, Corwin Springs, MT 59030-5000 or call 1-888-700-8087.

Appendix

LORD MICHAEL

In the name of the beloved mighty victorious Presence of God, I AM in me, my very own beloved Holy Christ Self, Holy Christ Selves of all mankind, beloved Archangel Michael, beloved Lanello, the entire Spirit of the Great White Brotherhood and the World Mother, elemental life—fire, air, water, and earth! I decree:

1. Lord Michael, Lord Michael,
   I call unto thee—
   Wield thy sword of blue flame
   And now cut me free!

Refrain: Blaze God-power, protection
   Now into my world,
   Thy banner of Faith
   Above me unfurl!
   Transcendent blue lightning
   Now flash through my soul,
   I AM by God's mercy
   Made radiant and whole!

2. Lord Michael, Lord Michael,
   I love thee, I do—
   With all thy great Faith
   My being imbue!

3. Lord Michael, Lord Michael
   And legions of blue—
   Come seal me, now keep me
   Faithful and true!

Coda: I AM with thy blue flame
   Now full-charged and blest,
   I AM now in Michael's
   Blue-flame armor dressed! (3x)

(continues)

And in full Faith I consciously accept this manifest, manifest, manifest! (3x) right here and now with full Power, eternally sustained, all-powerfully active, ever expanding, and world enfolding until all are wholly ascended in the Light and free!

Beloved I AM! Beloved I AM! Beloved I AM!

MICHAEL, ARCHANGEL OF FAITH

In the name of the beloved mighty victorious Presence of God, I AM in me, Holy Christ Selves of all mankind, beloved Archangel Michael and Faith, the seven beloved archangels and their divine complements, their legions of white-fire and blue-lightning angels, beloved Lanello, the entire Spirit of the Great White Brotherhood and the World Mother, elemental life—fire, air, water, and earth! I decree for a triple blue-ring protection around the students of the Ascended Masters, America, and the world:

1. O dearest Michael, archangel of Faith,
   Around my life protection seal;
   Let each new day my Faith increase
   That God in life is all that's real.

Refrain: Go before me, Michael dear,
   Thy shield of Faith I do revere;
   Armor of Light's living flame,
   Manifest action in God's name.

2. O Michael, Michael, Prince of Light,
   Angel of Faith, beautiful, bright:
   Around me now protection seal,
   Let heaven's Faith all error heal.

3. Michael, Michael, raise me now,
   To my God Self I will bow;
   Scintillating flame of Power,
   My vows do keep each blessed hour.

And in full Faith . . .

THE LAW OF FORGIVENESS

Beloved mighty victorious Presence of God, I AM in me, beloved Holy Christ Self, beloved Heavenly Father, beloved great Karmic Board, beloved Kuan Yin, Goddess of Mercy, beloved Lanello, the entire Spirit of the Great White Brotherhood and the World Mother, elemental life—fire, air, water, and earth!

In the name and by the power of the Presence of God which I AM and by the magnetic power of the sacred fire vested in me, I call upon the Law of Forgiveness and the Violet Transmuting Flame for each transgression of thy Law, each departure from thy sacred covenants.

Restore in me the Christ Mind, forgive my wrongs and unjust ways, make me obedient to thy code, let me walk humbly with thee all my days.

In the name of the Father, the Mother, the Son, and the Holy Spirit, I decree for all whom I have ever wronged and for all who have ever wronged me:

> Violet Fire,* enfold us! (3x)
> Violet Fire, hold us! (3x)
> Violet Fire, set us free! (3x)

> I AM, I AM, I AM surrounded by
>   a pillar of Violet Flame,*
> I AM, I AM, I AM abounding in
>   pure Love for God's great name,
> I AM, I AM, I AM complete
>   by thy pattern of Perfection so fair,
> I AM, I AM, I AM God's radiant flame
>   of Love gently falling through the air.

> Fall on us! (3x)
> Blaze through us! (3x)
> Saturate us! (3x)

And in full Faith . . .

---

* "Mercy's flame" or "purple flame" may be used for "violet flame" and "violet fire."

O VIOLET FLAME, FLOOD THE WORLD!

Great Cosmic Light, come forth and blaze here! Angelic hosts, come forth and blaze thy mighty Light rays through these, thy people!

Angels of Saint Germain and El Morya, come forth and blaze the will of God and the power of transmutation, in the holy name of Freedom, through this place and out into the world of form, until everyone upon earth feels a great release of the pressure of that substance known as sin and human discord from their worlds!

Erase and erase and *erase* the memory—cause, effect, and power—of these conditions from their beings, and let them enter the new world with a clean slate, wiped clean this night by the power of the Violet Flame!

O Violet Flame! O Violet Flame! O Violet Flame!
In the name of God, in the name of God, in the name of God!
O Violet Flame! O Violet Flame! O Violet Flame!
Flood the world! and *flood* the world! and *flood* the world!
In the I AM name, in the I AM name, in the I AM name!

Peace and Peace and Peace be spread throughout the earth!
May the Orient express Peace,
May the Occident express Peace,
May Peace come from the East and go to the West,
Come from the North and go to the South,
And circle the world around!
May the swaddling garments of the earth
Be in place to magnify the Lord
In this day and hour and this night.
May the world abide in an aura of God Peace!

Other titles from

SUMMIT UNIVERSITY ☙ PRESS®

Saint Germain's Prophecy for the New Millennium

Reincarnation: The Missing Link in Christianity

The Path to Your Ascension

Understanding Yourself

The Human Aura

The Lost Years of Jesus

The Lost Teachings of Jesus

Sacred Psychology of Love

Quietly Comes the Buddha

POCKET GUIDE
TO PRACTICAL SPIRITUALITY:

The Creative Power of Sound

Soul Mates and Twin Flames

Creative Abundance

How to Work with Angels

Access the Power of Your Higher Self

Violet Flame to Heal Body, Mind & Soul

Summit University Press titles are available from fine bookstores everywhere, including Barnes and Noble, B. Dalton Bookseller, Borders, Hastings and Waldenbooks.

To request a free catalog of books and tapes published by Summit University Press, write or call us at PO Box 5000, Corwin Springs, MT 59030-5000. Telephone 1-888-700-8087. Fax 1-800-221-8307 or 406-848-9555. E-mail: tslinfo@tsl.org Web site: www.tsl.org/supress